the
people
effect

JOEL CARVER & MARY M. WEBER

the
people
effect

FIND, GROW, AND RETAIN
THE BEST OF THE BEST

Advantage®

Published by Advantage, Charleston, South Carolina.
Member of Advantage Media Group.

ADVANTAGE is a registered trademark, and the Advantage colophon is a trademark of Advantage Media Group, Inc.

Printed in the United States of America.

10 9 8 7 6 5 4 3 2 1

ISBN: 978-1-64225-086-2
LCCN: 2019936323

Cover and layout design by Mary Hamilton.

This publication is designed to provide accurate and authoritative information in regard to the subject matter covered. It is sold with the understanding that the publisher is not engaged in rendering legal, accounting, or other professional services. If legal advice or other expert assistance is required, the services of a competent professional person should be sought.

Advantage Media Group is proud to be a part of the Tree Neutral® program. Tree Neutral offsets the number of trees consumed in the production and printing of this book by taking proactive steps such as planting trees in direct proportion to the number of trees used to print books. To learn more about Tree Neutral, please visit **www.treeneutral.com**.

Advantage Media Group is a publisher of business, self-improvement, and professional development books and online learning. We help entrepreneurs, business leaders, and professionals share their Stories, Passion, and Knowledge to help others Learn & Grow. Do you have a manuscript or book idea that you would like us to consider for publishing? Please visit **advantagefamily.com** or call **1.866.775.1696**.

To my Dad, who taught me to take risks. Even if you're not quite ready
for them, they might not present themselves again.
—Joel Carver

To my husband, David, whose patience and support enables me to
achieve my goals.
—Mary M. Weber

TABLE OF CONTENTS

ABOUT THE AUTHORS

Joel Carver and **Mary Weber** first crossed paths in 2008 when they both worked in senior leadership roles with a hospitality management and real estate company. At that point, Joel led the sales and marketing functions for the group and Mary was the senior HR leader for the organization. The journey that they went on—along with a team of great leaders—was first to keep the hotels profitable and staffed during the great recession, and second, to pivot to designing and implementing organizational strategies from recruitment and selection of the right people through compensation and training to create and support a team of associates that were among the best of the best in the hospitality industry as the economy recovered.

Mary moved on from that role to continue her thirty-year career in strategic human resources leadership and talent management strategies. She has combined practical, hands-on experience with solid best practices and theory as she returned to grad school and finished her masters in organizational leadership. She left the corporate world to consult, to provide leadership coaching, to teach at the collegiate level, and ultimately, to write this book to share her knowledge and experiences.

Joel also took the entrepreneurial path and founded The Carver Companies, which is transforming the hospitality industry as it has become the largest hospitality facing, human capital organization in North America.

Mary and Joel have continued to collaborate together to address human capital challenges facing each of them in their new roles. They have found a strong synergy in their perspectives and approaches to solve problems with strategic, creative, and pragmatic solutions that have, at the core, a deep respect for individual people and their differences.

This book was born out of the many comments that both Joel and Mary have heard from clients and colleagues saying: "You really need to write a book to share all of these experiences and perspectives." They heard it often enough that they decided—why not? Mary and Joel have seen a profound shift in how employers manage their employees and in how employees wish to be treated over this past decade. It is important that leaders take notice of this seismic change. So, here it is—a book that starts to share some of the foundational concepts they have found useful over their years in the hospitality industry and in managing and leading people. As dynamic leaders and change agents, both Joel and Mary are firm believers that whenever good people are involved, magic can happen.

FOREWORD

I have had the pleasure of working directly with Joel and Mary when I was president of CSM, a hotel and development company. Mary was the senior vice president of human resources and Joel was the senior vice president of sales and marketing.

During my time working with them, I found them both highly intuitive on human capital and the necessary man power to execute on a business plan. Joel was always far ahead of the competition with his thought processes to maximize sales and marketing in the hotel space, but he knew that he couldn't optimize his strategies without the right people. He and Mary worked closely together to gather the greatest minds to push revenues far beyond the competition, year after year using "out of the box" thought processes in conjunction with the latest technologies.

Two great minds have come together to share their secret sauce.

Rob Dann
EVP, Operations
Highgate Hotels

INTRODUCTION

The very essence of hospitality is about making people feel welcome and comfortable. Over the years, the hospitality industry has become proficient and even competitive in doing just that—providing a great guest experience. Hotels these days are going to personalize and tailor the guest experience to everyone's preferences. For example, when you're a guest in many hotels, you can often use self-check-in kiosks if you don't feel like interacting with a hotel employee at that moment. Otherwise, you can still have a Front Desk Agent handle everything for you. The metric of GSS (Guest Service Scores) was developed to ensure that hotels are accomplishing the objective of delighting their customers, and over the years, it's become one of the key metrics by which hotels judge their own success.

But a great guest experience doesn't just occur automatically. It depends heavily on the teams who provide it. These people make the magic happen. You can have the best, most updated hotel property in an ideal location with great amenities but if your team is subpar or unprofessional, it will not matter. The hotel will not be successful and guests won't want to come back! Conversely, a property that is kept clean and provides outstanding guest service—provided by great employees—is a place guests will want to return to (and they will tell their friends about the great customer service). The second hotel will maintain market share and grow in profitability. The first one won't. That difference only happens because of the employees.

But there's a problem. Hotel employees aren't doing well in many hotels these days. Turnover is high, complaints are growing louder, and performance too often meets only the bare minimum of professional standards—if that. And when employees aren't performing, these hotels are struggling.

Why is this happening? Because we have seen a significant shift in priorities over the years. While profitability has always been the end goal, in today's world, an exclusive focus on the P & L (profit and loss statement) seems to have taken over how many hotels are managed. The goal of every hotel is to provide a clean, well-run hotel with a great guest experience—profitably. However, recently the "profitably" part has been crowding out everything else! With the P & L driving most decisions, hotel managers have forgotten about the people effect. The guests and the employees have taken a total backseat to the bottom line. Sit in almost any P & L review meeting in any hotel or hotel group in the world, and all you'll hear about are line items. Our biggest assets and our biggest liabilities (our people) are literally never mentioned—unless it's to look at total payroll expenses!

During the great recession with its high unemployment, employees became a commodity. If one didn't work out, "move on and find another" was the norm. Guess what? It's been a full decade since then. That paradigm has shifted. National unemployment in the United States is at the lowest point in fifty years.[1] Talent has become a scarce resource. Good employees are harder and harder to

---

1   Aive Schneider, "U.S. Unemployment Rate Drops to 3.7 Percent, Lowest In Nearly 50 Years," *NPR*, October 5, 2018, https://www.npr.org/2018/10/05/654417887/u-s-unemployment-rate-drops-to-3-7-percent-lowest-in-nearly-50-years.

find, let alone retain. So, the recession-era way to view and treat them needs to change—and change fast.

Hotel operators, like other business owners, *must* shift from treating employees like commodities to treating them like the assets they are. The only way to attract and retain the best talent is to value the people who possess that talent and create a positive, memorable, and supportive employee experience for them.

Employees are the foundation of the success of any business—particularly in the hotel industry. If we treat our people well, they will treat our customers well, which will treat our P & L sheet well. If we don't, our guest experiences will collapse and take our profits with them.

In this book, the we share some best practices on how to create a strong and positive employee experience. We organized the flow of the book to mirror the experience that most employers have with their employees—beginning with the fundamentals like organizational culture, then moving through recruiting, selection, performance management, career development, etc. Most chapters are organized into two sections. First, you'll find a storyline illustrating some of the challenges associated with managing people in a complex hotel setting. The story we have imagined includes two important points of view: a general manager and an HR Director. If you're reading this book, you may likely share one of those points of view! While this book is primarily targeted to hoteliers, following the story of Margaret and Josh, the concepts and solutions presented here are tried and true and easily applied to many other industries.

The second section of each chapter will include ideas and best practices—solutions—that hotel GMs and HR managers can start using immediately to enhance the employee experience in their hotels. Our plan is not just to inspire and provide examples, but also to give concrete action steps and strategies. Finally, we have a section of samples and resources at the end of the book, so you won't have to reinvent the wheel to get started with any of the tactics we cover.

The goal in writing this book is to encourage and empower hotel owners and operators to begin dedicating the same attention and care to their greatest resources, their people, that they have previously dedicated to brick and mortar assets and line items on the P & L sheet. If you're on board with that goal, this book is for you.

CHAPTER ONE

THE STORY BEGINS

The Shift Hits the Fan

"Mr. Haversham, I know last quarter's numbers weren't where we wanted them, but—" Margaret paused as her asset manager cut her off for the third time in a ten-minute call.

As Haversham began railing again, Margaret looked helplessly at the ceiling, gritting her teeth in frustration. The call ended a few minutes later, with Margaret having said little more than "Yes, sir" and "I'll keep after it." Drained, Margaret looked at her watch—it wasn't even ten in the morning yet, and already the day was falling apart.

Her admin, Kimbr, entered the general manager's office of The Capitol House hotel with a soft knock, bearing the agenda sheets for that day's staff meeting.

"That sounded like it could have gone better," said Kimbr with sympathy. "I couldn't make out much from my desk, but Haversham usually lets you talk more than that."

"You're telling me," said Margaret, glaring at the phone. "I'd like to see him come down here and do better than we're doing. He's only been our asset manager for three years. I've been GM here almost fifteen! And front desk manager before that, and desk clerk before that—ugh!" Margaret threw up her hands.

Kimbr nodded. "I know. But you said so yourself before he called—Capitol House is struggling. Did he give you any actual advice in there, or just yell?"

"Oh, he told me plenty of things to do, starting with talking to Josh again! As if some twenty-eight-year-old *kid* knows more about handling my employees than I do! No, I've turned us around before, I can do it again. I just need time."

"Did he give you any?" asked Kimbr.

"I've got six months to stabilize things and start showing growth again. After that . . ." Margaret sighed. "He didn't say in so many words, but it'll probably be my job. So no, he didn't give me time—not enough, anyway."

Kimbr thought for a moment, then took a different tack. "What's really bothering you about Josh?"

"Well, for starters, he wants to change everything about human resources! We can't say this, we can't do that, we have to post on social media, we have to engage our team members ... when I started here, we could just place an ad for the person we needed, hire them, tell them what to do, and if they didn't cut it, fire them! It's not that hard, and it's worked for years. Why do we have to change it?

"And he's so focused on telling me what we need to do differently that he's not doing what he should! I walked in here this morning and there was a new house person dusting the lobby who looked like she'd slept in her uniform! We can't have employees look that sloppy at work. Josh should have made that clear when he and

Dolores hired her. Maybe if he spent more time making our people look professional and less time worrying about that Glass Window thing, we'd actually start making some progress."

"I think you mean Glassdoor," Kimbr ventured.

"Door, window, whatever! The point is, he needs to be doing his job, not telling me how to do mine." Margaret locked eyes with her young admin, daring her to disagree.

Kimbr held her boss's gaze, used to Margaret's outbursts in moments of stress. After a few moments, Margaret sagged back into her desk chair.

"That isn't all you're upset about, is it." Kimbr's voice was gentle, but she made it a statement rather than a question.

Margaret looked up, seeming suddenly smaller. "It's all going out of control, Kimbr. I used to have a handle on everything, but now I feel like I'm just trying to hold on by my fingernails. And the more I try to make sure everything's working, the less it all seems to work. I'm proud of this hotel, and I don't want to lose it. But if I can't turn things around in six months, I don't know if there will be a Capitol House anymore, let alone a place for me as its GM. And I don't know if I can make that happen." She looked down, absently shuffling papers across the desktop.

Kimbr said nothing, knowing this was the root of her boss's struggles.

"What should I do?" Margaret's voice was quiet now, almost inaudible. "You've been with me eight years, Kimbr, you know enough of my responsibilities. What would you do if you were me?"

"You won't like it."

"Tell me anyway."

"After the staff meeting, let me talk to Josh. If I can convince him to ease up on beating the change-everything-all-at-once drum, will you listen to some of his suggestions?"

Margaret rubbed her temples, hoping her rising headache would go away. "You really think he can help with this situation?"

"I've talked to him a few times. He's pretty sharp—he's gotten good results at three other hotels at lower-level positions, and I think he really cares about Capitol House. I'd give him one more chance—and I'd really *listen* to him this time."

Margaret was silent for a long moment. Then she said, "Alright. Talk to him. If he has ideas to turn our numbers around in six months, I'll listen to them."

The two women rose and headed for the staff meeting.

Two hours later, Josh managed not to slam the door as he stormed into his office, but it was a close thing.

I don't believe this! he thought. *I asked that those items be added to the staff meeting agenda two weeks ago! And Margaret mentions one for about three seconds and completely skips the other two! This is ridiculous. It's like I have no intelligence or credibility or experience in her eyes. I should never have taken this job.*

A light knock on the door made him jump. He turned to see Kimbr, who had apparently followed him back from the staff meeting.

"What?" he snapped before he could stop himself.

Kimbr raised an eyebrow, but only said, "Margaret asked me to talk to you."

"About what? Maybe about how my agenda items didn't make it into the staff meeting?" Josh took a deep breath to center himself. "Sorry. That was uncalled for. What did she want you to tell me?"

"That she's willing to hear you out on a few things."

Josh barked a skeptical laugh. "Really? After three months of 'that's not how we do things around here!' she's changing her tune? Why does that smell fishy from her?" He dropped into his chair, waving Kimbr to take a seat herself.

Kimbr closed the door and sat down across from Josh. "Look, I know this sounds like I'm blowing smoke, but I'm serious. Margaret had a call with Mr. Haversham this morning, and I think something finally got through to her. She knows some things have to change, and she's willing to hear your suggestions. Did you see how she was at the staff meeting? She's two steps away from an anxiety attack. That's probably why she skipped two of your agenda items. And besides, talking to you today wasn't all Haversham's idea. It was mine, too."

That made Josh look up in surprise. "Your idea? Why?"

Kimbr leaned forward and met Josh's eyes. "I see what's happening here. If you two keep refusing to work together, the hotel's probably going to go under. I'm pretty sure you and Margaret don't want that, and I don't want it either. But I've watched you both. You care about Capitol House. Margaret cares about Capitol House. If you two got on the same page, you could turn things around for the hotel. Make it the kind of high-profile draw it was twenty years ago, only today. If Margaret listens to you, that's a step in the right direction."

Josh nodded slowly. "So what, you're on my side now?"

Kimbr shook her head. "I'm on the hotel's side. And that means you need to listen to Margaret, too. She may seem behind the times to you, but she's not stupid. So don't just tell her to change because you say so. Help her understand how your ideas can help the hotel. She'll respond well to that."

"You really think so?"

"I wouldn't have convinced Margaret to let me talk to you if I didn't."

Josh leaned back and stared at the ceiling. Kimbr waited.

Finally, Josh gave a decisive nod. "Okay. I'm still skeptical, but I'll give this one more try. Maybe if Margaret and I can listen to each other, we can start to build some trust and make some actual progress."

Kimbr smiled and then stood up to leave. "I was hoping you'd say that. She's waiting for you in her office now."

Josh grabbed a folder of notes and followed Kimbr into the hall.

CHAPTER TWO

IT'S ALL ABOUT CULTURE AND EX!

The Story

Margaret looked up as Josh stepped into her office. Josh was surprised to see more fear than the usual irritation in his boss's eyes. The two looked at each other for a moment, not saying anything. Finally Josh ventured, "Kimbr said you wanted to hear some of my suggestions again?"

Margaret nodded, pointing to a chair. Josh raised his eyebrows but sat down.

"Josh, I'm going to level with you. Capitol House is not doing well. Two years ago, we began to see a decline in employee morale. Then, eighteen months ago, our turnover rate started to increase, which coincided with our declining GSS scores. Then, our occupancy started to decline, so we started lowering rates to combat that, which promptly translated into lower revenues and, well, you know the rest. Now, profitability is in the toilet. We have six months to get things back on an even keel. I need you to help me do that. Can I count on you?" Margaret's voice was clipped, her tone short.

Josh thought for a moment. "Margaret, if you're asking me to do what I can to help save this hotel, of course you can count on me. But if you're asking me to just do what I'm told and keep my mouth shut, I can't do that. I'm here right now because Kimbr told me you were willing to listen to me. If that's not actually true, then I don't see a way forward for us."

"I do want to hear your suggestions," said Margaret. "Here, we'll start with our GSS scores. They're down. Still. How would you suggest we get them back up? And here's another thing. Not a single employee I saw on the floor today was smiling. A couple didn't even look up as I walked by! That's unacceptable—Both of these issues are your responsibility. How do you suggest we fix them?"

Josh leaned back, rolling his eyes. "Alright, let's assume for the moment that I am fully responsible for everything you just described. If I were, the first thing I'd ask is whether our employees understand that it is our expectation that they look up and greet anyone they encounter during the day. Maybe they didn't smile at you because they didn't know it was expected of them as employees of Capitol House. Are you *sure* those folks you saw today were clear on those expectations?"

Margaret looked up sharply. "Seriously? You're the HR Director doing the hiring! It's your job to know the answers to questions like that. If you have to ask, maybe you're in the wrong job!"

"If you only want employees who never ask questions, you're not letting me *do* my job!" Josh shot back. "No wonder our GSS score is so low!"

"Stop it, both of you!" came Kimbr's voice from the still-open doorway. The usually calm admin looked ready to chew nails. She stepped inside and closed the door, looking first at Margaret, then at Josh. "Look, I know this is over my head, but I love this hotel as much as either of you do. Write me up if you have to, but I will not let you two kill the hotel because you can't work together. Margaret, you told me two hours ago that you were willing to *listen* to Josh, not yell at him. And Josh, you told me not ten minutes ago that you would try not to get defensive and sarcastic. Now both of you need to do what you said you'd do and work together, or so help me I will apply at the Ritz-Carlton!" Message delivered, Kimbr turned on her heel and walked out of the office.

Josh and Margaret stared after her. After a few moments, Josh turned back to his boss.

"She's right. I didn't need to be so sarcastic, and I'm sorry," he said.

Margaret swallowed hard but met his eyes and nodded. "I'm sorry, too. I know I'm frustrated, but I shouldn't take it out on you. We wouldn't choose this path for a day in the park, but like it or not, it's the path we're on and we're on it together. Let me start again. What did you mean about people not knowing their expectations?"

"Well, while you and I have a very clear picture of what we want our hotel to be like, maybe we have not done an adequate job clarifying that picture to our employees. We assume that the team shares our perspective, but you know what they say about people who make assumptions!"

Margaret nodded and gestured for Josh to continue.

"A lot of this boils down to creating a culture of support and service. I'm not sure that we've done a great job with defining our culture and communicating it to the team. If our people don't get how they fit into our culture, or how the culture supports them, it doesn't surprise me that they don't communicate or provide that culture to our guests. That may be at the root of why our GSS scores are so low."

"Hmm," Margaret thought for a moment before responding. "I've been reading about the importance of a good company culture lately. I probably haven't spent enough time thinking about that for the hotel and I sure as heck know that we don't talk about it enough. Maybe that is a place to start our work."

"Well, our exit interview comments sure seem to indicate that our employees would not rate our culture very high," Josh noted. "I'm not actually sure that I could define our culture if someone asked me to. I guess we can't enforce a culture when we can't even describe it or let our employees know what is expected."

"Agreed. Is this something you could take a crack at?"

Josh nodded. "I did participate in this kind of exercise with my last hotel. The entire senior leadership team met for an offsite planning meeting. We did some group work with flipcharts and defined the mission, vision, and values of the hotel. Then we used all of that as the basis for employee communications and for defining performance expectations. I had completely forgotten about that till this morning, but it did provide a pretty good foundation for managing the culture of the hotel."

Margaret grabbed a pen and began scribbling notes. "I think we may be on to something here! You know, the feel of this place used to be really special—people *wanted* to work here. I don't really know when that changed. I think this might give us a chance to better understand the perspectives of each of the hotel leaders AND to make sure we are all on the same page. We sure aren't right now!"

Josh was picking up on Margaret's growing excitement. "Okay, as long as we are talking about working on our culture, let me take this one step further. I think we need to go beyond the hotel culture and create an actual employee experience."

Margaret stopped writing. "An employee experience? You lost me there. Is that like a guest experience, but for our workers?"

"Exactly," said Josh. "You know, the big buzz in the past few years in marketing has been the 'customer experience' or 'CX.' So this is along the same lines. I learned a lot about it at the HR conference I went to last month. We'll call it the 'employee experience'—the EX."

Josh grabbed a piece of paper from Margaret's desk and began listing points. "Because the labor market is so tight these days, smart employers are paying attention to the total experience that their employees have at work, not just how much they get paid or how many hours they work. The focus seems to be on three key areas: First, enhancing the physical work environment; second, using technology in a smart way; and third, defining and articulating the culture of the organization. In short, we have to care about our employees as much as we care about our customers. While we are doing some planning with the team, maybe we can talk more about where we are already doing a good job and where we can get better in our employee experience." He spun the sheet around so Margaret could read what he'd written.

"I'll be honest, Josh, it sounds like a lot of new stuff to deal with, and I'm not quite sure how this will turn everything around for us. My instinct is to say no. But I'm realizing I'm out of my depth here. As much as I hate to admit it, you know more about this than I do. And besides, our backs are against the wall. Our next senior management meeting is next week. Let's put something together about culture and employee experience for that meeting, and we'll see how it goes. And I promise it won't get accidentally dropped from the agenda this time. Fair enough?"

"Fair enough," Josh said, a little dazed from Margaret's change in attitude but not about to object. "I'll put together some notes for a presentation and have them on your desk tomorrow."

As Josh left the office and walked past Kimbr, he could've sworn he saw her smiling into her coffee.

The Solution

CULTURE MATTERS

Leadership guru Peter Drucker once stated that "Culture eats strategy for breakfast."[2] Good organizational culture is critical to attracting and retaining the best talent *and* to achieving the desired business results. Make no mistake, your hotel already has a culture, whether you know it or not. This culture may be helping you, or it may be hurting you.

What do we mean by organizational culture? We define culture as the values, beliefs, customs, and rules that apply in your hotel. Your culture will influence how you lead, how your employees work, and ultimately, the experience for your guests. Your culture will be demonstrated by how your employees feel about their work, their colleagues, and the hotel itself.

Some franchise hotel groups may feel that key elements of their culture are dictated by the brand of that hotel. This is logical, as many brands mandate what employees wear, how they are groomed, and how they interact with guests. A few actually have a signature "scent" for the hotel that signifies their unique guest experience and evokes happiness and delight. Some brands also have required language that employees must use with guests like "It's my pleasure,"

---

2   "Culture eats strategy for breakfast," The Management Centre, https://www. managementcentre.co.uk/culture-eats-strategy-for-breakfast.

"Be our guest," or, "Yes, I can." These requirements contribute to the culture, creating a unique environment for employees that no other hotel brand will duplicate.

But brand requirements are only the beginning of a hotel's culture. For one thing, the management company may have their own "secret sauce" on top of the brand requirements. Management companies may provide guidance on job descriptions, pay ranges, work shifts, and performance criteria, as well as expectations for employee performance. These will all have an impact on the employee experience and the culture.

Most importantly, each hotel will have its own culture that is representative of both the leadership team and the demographics of the employee group. That is, the people themselves will create the culture by their backgrounds, their personality traits, their perspectives, and their approaches to work—not to mention their leadership styles, when applicable. The challenge is, this culture will show up in your hotel whether or not you design it.

A well-designed and well-communicated culture will take all of these diverse approaches and guide them to work together and create positive results. A poorly designed culture, or one that hasn't been designed at all, will let all the diverse people pretty much do whatever they want—which leads to a haphazard and potentially problematic culture. Similarly, if leaders don't clearly articulate their expectations for employee behavior and how it fits into the greater hotel culture (to each other and to guests), then they cannot be surprised or distressed when that behavior does not happen and the culture falls apart.

Understand that your hotel will have its own unique culture—it is just a matter of whether you drive it or it drives you.

To drive your culture, we suggest every hotel do the following.

DEFINE THE HOTEL'S MISSION AND VISION

Mission and vision are important cornerstones of every organization's culture. While the two are closely related, they each serve a slightly different purpose—mission determines who you are, whereas vision clarifies where you want to go—and are both essential.

In order to develop these, the hotel leader should convene the senior leadership group (you may also want to consider including a small number of forward-thinking, functional leaders in your hotel) and define who you are as an organization—what does your hotel stand for? What words describe how you want the hotel to be perceived? Use a whiteboard or flipchart and just have the group throw out suggestions for several minutes. This exercise provides insight into the perspectives of the key leaders and what is important to each person. Your team will find synergy around some core concepts and words that come up during this brainstorm, which can then be expanded, combined, and built on to draft a mission statement and a vision (e.g., What does "exceptional" mean in regard to guest service? What does it mean to be an industry leader?). One result of this planning session should be a draft of both mission and vision statements.

Mission statements can be helpful to define who you are as an organization and what distinguishes you from others. What does your hotel do—why do you exist? Who do you serve and how specifically do you serve them? Your mission may be something like: "To provide an outstanding guest experience to businesses and other travelers." Marriott Hotel's mission statement is, "*To enhance the lives of our customers by creating and enabling unsurpassed vacation and leisure experiences.*"

The vision statement—usually shorter and more aspirational— is about where you are going as a hotel. This is what we want to be in the future. The vision tends to be what excites the employees and makes them feel that they are part of something bigger.

The Walt Disney vision statement is a great example of this.

"To make people happy."

This phrase is an invitation for like-minded employees to join the team. Who wouldn't want to work there to be part of making this come true?

Marriott International's vision statement is:

"To become the premiere provider and facilitator of leisure & vacation experiences in the world."

Words like "premiere" send a distinct message about how the brand wants to be seen.

Hilton Hotels want:

"To fill the earth with the light and warmth of hospitality."

This highly aspirational statement is intended to set the tone for their facilities.

Keep both statements short so that they can easily be remembered and repeated. Communicate them often so that you continue to reinforce their importance. And, finally, make them the basis of all of your strategic decisions so that they drive your business and are not just words on a piece of paper.

ESTABLISH CORE VALUES

Core values are an essential component of defining organizational culture. The stated values serve as compass for the actions of both leaders and employees. The values define how you want each and every employee to behave each and every day. Leaders *must* walk the talk with the values, demonstrating them and helping their employees work with them—otherwise, they become empty words.

Your core values can also emerge out of the focused brainstorming session with your leaders that creates your mission statement and vision (or they can be the subject of a separate session). Most hotels will do well with five to seven core values.

We've included examples both from a hotel company and from a well-known cultural icon to demonstrate that while the styles differ, these organizations and industries all recognize the importance of defining and communicating these core values.

IKEA has done a nice job of defining their core values in a simple and compelling way. As a customer, it's easy to see how these core values are demonstrated—the stores certainly do exist to be cost effective and innovative. Their values clearly support those goals:

- Humbleness and willpower

- Leadership by example

- Daring to be different

- Togetherness and enthusiasm

- Cost-consciousness

- Constant desire for renewal

- Accept and delegate responsibility.

Google has ten core values, which may be too many for most organizations—it is hard for the employees to remember when there are too many. However, we like the straightforward language that they use:

- Focus on the user and all else will follow.

- It's best to do one thing really, really well.

- Fast is better than slow.

- Democracy on the web works.

- You don't need to be at your desk to need an answer.

- You can make money without doing evil.

- There's always more information out there.

- The need for information crosses all borders.

- You can be serious without a suit.

- Great just isn't good enough.

Hilton Brands lay out a simple group of six values that reflect their desire to lead the hotel industry in both guest experience and good reputation. They also take their values to a new level by adding some branding, which will certainly help employees to remember them:

H. Hospitality. We're passionate about delivering exceptional guest experiences.

I. Integrity. We do the right thing, all the time.

L. Leadership. We're leaders in our industry and in our communities.

T. Teamwork. We're team players in everything we do.

O. Ownership. We're the owners of our actions and decisions.

N. Now. We operate with a sense of urgency and discipline.

CREATE A CODE OF CONDUCT

Some hotels find it helpful to take the definition of their culture one more step by adding a Code of Conduct. This document, which is provided to every employee upon being hired (maybe even during the interview phase), is a guide to putting the hotel's values into action the right way.

This document can be helpful because some employees will interpret your values differently than you intended. This isn't usually a personal failing or even a conscious decision on the employee's part—instead, it's simply the result of an easily filled knowledge gap. Hotels often employ a large number of entry level workers who may not have much relevant professional work experience (and, thus, not know exactly what it means, for instance, to bring a value such as integrity or responsibility to their job). As Josh mentioned in our story, it is often helpful to be crystal clear about your expectations so everyone knows up front what success looks like. A Code of Conduct helps you do that.

This document should be straightforward and fairly specific. It can cover everything from how uniforms should be worn and maintained, to cell phone usage on the job, to how to greet a guest in the hallway. We have attached a sample Code of Conduct for hotels in the Resources & Samples portion of the book—section 2.1.

COMMUNICATIONS ARE KEY

It is all well and good for leadership to participate in this thinking exercise and to define these key items. However, the importance of the rollout and on-going communication of these tools *cannot* be overstated. A strong organizational culture is one that is based on every employee having the information they need in order to do their job successfully. We cannot emphasize enough that regular communication updates—whether it is weekly staff meetings, team meetings, daily huddles, or periodic town hall meetings—can all be critical components of making sure that everyone is on the same page.

Talk to your employees about mission, vision, and values often. Post them on the break room walls and in other workspaces your employees move through often. Build them into your branding so your customers know to expect them—and your employees know the customers expect them! Integrate these concepts into new employee orientation, into the performance management tools, and into all employee training programs. Center your employee recognition programs on the demonstration of your core values.

Now, we realize that this is the point where some of you readers will roll your eyes and say that you need to run a hotel and not sit in tons of useless and time-consuming meetings. You are correct— tons of long, tedious meeting are a waste of time. However, when leaders focus on short, impactful meetings that have clear agendas and defined outcomes—it will not waste anyone's time but will add value and ultimately save time.

Effective meeting guidelines include:

- Have a stated purpose or outcome for every meeting.

- Determine who needs to be in the meeting and why. There should be a role for every participant—not just because they "might want to know what is going on." You can always update them after the meeting.

- Draft an agenda and send it out in advance to allow participants to review and consider before the meeting.

- Add approximate times for each discussion to the agenda— that will help you decide if you are trying to do too much in one meeting (a common problem) and will help to keep you on track.

- If it is a standing meeting—consider defining some basic ground rules to make the time productive. This can include starting and ending on time, no mobile phones allowed, etc.

- As a facilitator, make sure that only one person talks at a time, no interrupting others and no side conversations are happening to divert the focus.

Written communications or visual reminders of expectations, core values, etc., are also important. Different people learn in different ways, so it is important to respond to the visual learners, as well. Newsletters, email updates, posters, etc., can all be effective tools for communication. Remember that the new generations of workers are extremely visual, so the more graphical the communication, the better. Pictures truly do speak a thousand words.

The bottom line here is that, as Margaret and Josh discussed, if we do not tell employees what behaviors we expect, the only thing we can expect is that we won't get it—and if we don't build the culture we want and welcome our employees into it, the culture that forms instead will be one that doesn't help our hotel (and may, in fact, hurt it).

EMPLOYEE EXPERIENCE

How leaders treat their employees is an embodiment of their values and a true indicator of their organizational culture. The best cultures are those where the employees are valued and respected. The sum of all of the interactions that an organization has with an employee is holistically called the "employee experience." A recent Forbes Magazine article noted that this should be such a focus for employers that they called 2018 *The Year of Employee Experience.* The author, Denise Lee Yon, notes that employee experience (EX) is every employee interaction, from the first contact as a potential recruit to the last interaction after the end of employment.[3]

Note that these activities are not the same as employee engagement, which is the OUTCOME of all of the work done to enhance the employee experience. Creating and supporting a positive work culture is fundamental to creating a great employee experience.

3   Denise Lee Yohn, "2018 Will Be the Year of Employee Experience," *Forbes,* January 2, 2018, https://www.forbes.com/sites/deniselyohn/2018/01/02/2018-will-be-the-year-of-employee-experience/#26a7bf581c8f.

CHAPTER THREE

THE CRACK IN THE GLASS DOOR

The Story

"Alright, Josh," said Margaret. "I've read over your ideas for a staff meeting about culture and core values, and I think it could be a good start. But I'm concerned that's all it will be—and I'm worried a good start just won't be enough."

The two were back in Margaret's office a few days later, and both the stacks of STR® (Smith Travel Research) trend report and other documents covering the desk (one stained brown by spilled coffee) and Margaret's strained expression told Josh that his boss was not having a great day. Not that he'd been having one himself—the Capitol House's newest Glassdoor reviews were terrible. Clearly, the hotel had a pretty bad rep to overcome as a difficult place to work.

"Why do you say that?" he asked. "We have to start or we'll never get anywhere."

"Well, sure, I know that," said Margaret. "But once we start, how do we keep going? You know as well as I do that one meeting isn't going to fix everything. Everyone will be excited for a few days, but then they'll just go back to doing what they always do, because it's what they've always done."

Josh nodded. "I hear you—and you're right, just having a meeting won't be enough. You know, what you just said reminds me of Einstein's definition of insanity."

"Einstein's what? You lost me there."

"Einstein's definition of insanity is doing the same thing over and over again and expecting different results," Josh said. "I love that concept and think it applies to our situation—we can't just try to do the same things in a different culture, we have to step back and look at how we do just about everything."

Margaret laughed. "Okay, I guess I asked for that with all the times I told you, 'We've never done it that way.' Where do we start on being less insane?"

"Well, for starters, as I reviewed some of the most recent Glassdoor comments, I noticed a theme about inefficient and old-school processes, and that the employees who left did not feel that their opinions were heard or respected. Workers who came up with new ideas or solutions to problems got lip-service answers or were told to just do what the boss told them to."

Margaret frowned. "But isn't it the leadership team's job to know the answers and come up with the solutions? Employees don't have the experience to do that yet, or else they can't see the big picture the way we can!"

Josh looked at Margaret for a long moment. "Margaret," he said, finally, "I really want to challenge you on that idea. For one thing, our workers are usually closer to problems than we are. There's no reason that their ideas to solve them couldn't be as good or better than the ones we come up with. And even if their answers aren't the best ones, why wouldn't we want to hear them anyway? Who knows, we might learn a thing or two ourselves. Either way, thinking that we have, or need to have, all the answers, is a big part of our problem here—and I don't just mean with Glassdoor. Wouldn't you agree?" He glanced meaningfully at the stack of STR reports.

Margaret sighed. "Yes, I suppose that's part of why we're talking about turning things around in the first place. Okay, let's say we want to give our employees a chance to help solve problems. How would we even do that? I hope you aren't going to suggest putting a housekeeper or bartender in my office for a day—I *know* that won't work!"

Josh grinned. "No, I was thinking about a system called Lean I learned about at my last hotel. Lean is a process of continuous improvement, where the goal is to approach running the hotel not as something we get right once and then never think about again, but something we're constantly working on and making better. One of the coolest things about it was that we, as leaders, don't need to have all the answers. We pull together teams of employees to help identify both the problems and the solutions. These 'Kaizen' or 'Lean' teams ensure that the team members are invested in the ideas as well as the leaders."

"I think I've heard about Lean before," said Margaret, "but I'm not sure how that will help us. Isn't that just for manufacturing? And what is this Kaizen thing that you mentioned?"

"Lean and Kaizen started in manufacturing," replied Josh, "but lots of other industries are using the concept now. Healthcare has gotten into it in a big way. Kaizen is one of the tools that makes Lean work—it is a focused, disciplined approach to tackling a smaller problem. It helps to break the work into bite-sized chunks. Lean may give us a place to start—an approach to use."

"Before we run forward," Margaret paused, "it just feels like the very last thing we need around here is another committee. Or am I just being cranky because you're making me change things?"

For the first time, Josh let loose a truly honest laugh. "I can't blame you for that; I'd rather have a root canal! You're dead on—we don't need another 'committee.' What we need is a group of folks that are open minded and forward thinking who can help us walk through the process, understand where we're having roadblocks, and look for new and creative solutions. Kaizen is not designed to support standing committees—rather more like short term SWAT teams to look at and solve specific problems. What we don't need is a group of 'Debbie Downers' sitting around moaning about what's wrong!"

Margaret nodded, gesturing for Josh to continue.

"Another key outcome of Lean is the focus on improvement—not perfection. I bet you've seen this situation a few times—where nothing ever gets done because a team is trying to make some new change perfect. This process helps folks understand that the goal is making things better—making forward progress. We don't strive for perfection, because it's not possible. We make it a little better and then keep working on it to make it even better and better—you get the idea."

Margaret sighed. She could feel the stress in her clenched jaw and tight shoulders. "Okay, Einstein, I think this could be worth a try. Now walk me through what we need to do to get this jump-started."

"We should work with the leaders to first identify a few discrete problems or work-flows that are not working well, and plan to assign a Kaizen team to each one. Next, we need to identify who we want to be on each Kaizen team—and who wants to be on them. One of the key things I learned at my old hotel was to make sure we have folks who can understand the value of working through the process. The GM was always so sure he knew the answer that he'd jump all the way over the process to his 'solution.' You'd be amazed how many times he had to admit he missed something, because he didn't allow the Kaizen process to actually happen."

Margaret nodded. "I know, I know—there's a lesson for me in that example, too, right?"

Josh grinned. "You said it, not me. But does that sound like a good starting point?"

"Yes, definitely," said Margaret. "Let's include this on the agenda for the culture and core values meeting, maybe during the second half, and see what we come up with."

The Solution

While process improvement—finding ways to eliminate waste and to be more efficient—has frequently provided a competitive advantage for organizations, it's now not just an option but a necessity. While process improvement has been used in the past to reduce the need for a large number of employees, the amount of work that must be today done is so massive that there simply aren't enough workers to do it all. Hotels must find better ways to get that work done with fewer employees, or they will not survive.

So, what is process improvement? It is a system of focused efforts designed to improve targeted work processes. It includes four steps:

1. Identifying opportunities for improvement (what's not working well right now?)

2. Defining a desired future state (how will things change to make them work well?)

3. Implementing changes (what can we do to start changing those things?)

4. Measuring the impact of those changes (what results occurred from making those changes?)

These steps are performed in repeated sequence—that is, once you finish the fourth step, you go back and start again with the first. That way, improvement truly becomes a constant cycle over time. Note that each cycle is focused on progress, not perfection—because there is no true end to continuous improvement, there is no need to "get it right the first time" or achieve perfection on only one cycle. Instead, the goal is to improve gradually but continuously, so that over time, things get better and better.

It's helpful to maintain a structured approach, uniform tools, and a common language around these steps of continuous improvement. It can be difficult to get people's focus off of "their day jobs" and to keep momentum and focus on improvement tactics. These tools will help employees to find the needed discipline.

There are a number of different approaches to continuous improvement that include these uniform structures, tools, and language. One of the most effective is the "Lean" system. While this methodology started in manufacturing, its applications have become widespread. The term "lean" was coined to describe Toyota's business during the late 1980s and is easily translated to the world of hospitality. We particularly like the two basic pillars of beliefs that Lean defined.

1. All work is a process, and all processes can be improved. This means that everything that we do in our hotels is actually a process that we can see, map, and ultimately make better.

2. Good ideas come from those who are performing the work.

Kaizen (the supporting tool for Lean that Josh talked about) includes a concept called *Gemba*, which means "going to where the work happens." In other words, respect and involve your employees in the process of continuous improvement and you will find the best solutions.

The Japanese process of *Kaizen* (roughly translates to "good change") is a long-term approach to work that systematically seeks to achieve small, incremental changes in processes in order to improve efficiency and quality. The simple act of working through the Kaizen process often brings us to an "aha moment."

Kaizen generates small improvements as a result of coordinated, continuous efforts by all employees. *Kaizen events* bring together a group of process owners and managers to map out an existing process and identify improvements that are within the scope of the participants.

Some basic Lean concepts include:

- Creating an internal *culture* of continuous improvement, cost containment, and change. Kaizen is not a one-time event.

- Process improvement focuses on making things better—not just fighting fires.

- Kaizen focuses on eliminating waste—of money, materials, time, and opportunities.

- Visual management = if you can't see it, you can't measure it or improve it (timelines, charts, diagrams). Keep score and make it visual.

- Value Stream Mapping—physically map out processes, data, and people involved. This helps you really *see* problems and identify bottlenecks and inefficiencies and work them out.

- Five Whys—when determining "why" a process step is done or if it is important, ask "why" five times to get to the root cause of a problem. Don't accept "because we've always done it that way" answers.

- Think about HOW one can improve versus WHY it cannot be done.

- Take immediate action—don't wait for perfection. Aim for 50 percent improvement and then do it again and again. Just do it.

We want to further expand on the last point above. Too often, people or organizations get "analysis paralysis." They want to have all the answers before doing anything. This is NOT a good approach. You will never have all the answers. Kaizen encourages making some small improvements now over full or complete improvements later —any positive change is better than none.

Supporting that, we often use the phrase *"Don't let great get in the way of good."* Many people struggle to implement good change because they can't stop asking, *"What if we can do it better?"* Then, nothing gets accomplished, because they are always looking for perfection, when the first simple action would have produced a much better outcome just by starting to make changes in the first place.

The technique that Kaizen uses to simplify work is summarized in the following four bullets and graphic.

- **Plan**—devise how to do it

- **Do**—run the process—test the proposal

- **Check**—evaluate the results

- **Act**—implement the idea

James P. Womack and Daniel T. Jones, *Lean Thinking: Banish Waste and Create Wealth in Your Corporation* (New York: Free Press, 2003).

CHAPTER FOUR

THE INVITATION

The Story

Josh sat down at his desk and smiled to himself. For the first time in several months, he was starting to feel pretty darn happy about working with Margaret. The leadership meeting about culture, mission, vision, and values they had co-facilitated had gone surprisingly well, with lots of energy and creative ideas from nearly all of the hotel leaders. In the two weeks since then, the hotel staff had seemed fairly receptive to the ideas their leaders had come up with. Many had offered their own suggestions, and several workers across multiple departments had volunteered to join Kaizen teams.

Margaret stuck her head into Josh's office with a quick tap on the door to announce herself.

"Josh, did you get a chance to synthesize all of the comments that we got about our core values? It was pretty cool how we arrived at five words that everyone seemed to get behind so quickly." Margaret smiled. "I think that **service**, **innovation**, **quality**, **integrity**, and **fun** really capture who we are—or want to be, anyway."

"Definitely," said Josh. "I think the leadership team has really started to rally around our culture work, and I can already see some of the employees starting to buy in. I'm really happy with our initial progress."

"Same here," said Margaret. "I wanted to follow up with you on the rest of the leadership team for a minute. Are they all still on board with everything now that we're a couple weeks out?"

Josh considered his words for a moment. "I'd say yes ... and no. Mark from Food and Beverage, Tiana from Front Desk, Dolores from Housekeeping, and Linh from Sales all seem like they're still on board—there have been a few stumbles, but nothing major. Billy from Engineering, though . . . I'm concerned about him."

"Why, what's the matter with him?"

Josh looked pointedly at the open door but said nothing. Margaret got the hint and closed it, then sat across from her HR Director.

Josh leaned forward to meet her eyes. "Billy has had a negative attitude about these ideas from the start, just like he has a negative attitude about anything he doesn't like. Did you hear him in the leadership meeting? 'This touchy-feely stuff is a total waste of time!' Not gonna lie, just between you and me, I wanted to smack him one for that. And when I followed up with him earlier this week, he just brushed me off, saying he had more important things to do."

"Billy's always been stubborn, sure, and his people skills aren't the strongest, but he's the best chief engineer this hotel's had since I started working here," said Margaret. "I'm sure he'll come around eventually."

Josh gave her a sharp look. "Maybe, but I'm not holding my breath. Remember how Jose, his assistant chief, was so excited to be on one of our Kaizen teams? This morning he told me Billy wouldn't let him participate anymore. He told Jose to just focus on his 'own job' and not try to fix things for other departments. Jose was really upset and disappointed. I really hope we don't lose him over this—he is a great guy and a good worker."

Margaret's eyebrows went up. "That's not good. I'll talk to Billy—maybe I can convince him to let Jose rejoin the Kaizen team."

"That would be great," said Josh. "But I'm not sure that's going to solve the problem. Look, Engineering has the second-highest turnover rate in this hotel, and that's only because Housekeeping always has the highest, due to the nature of the job. I have more complaints from Billy's employees than from any other department. He's openly critical with them all the time. And most of the other leadership team members can't stand him. I'm pretty sure he and Tiana have been feuding since she took over Front Desk three years ago, though that was before I got here, and you and I both know how easygoing she is."

"That's true," said Margaret. "I've talked with him multiple times about his attitude and told him not to openly and publicly criticize the other team members. While I realize I have some challenges when it comes to giving constructive feedback, I really do feel like I have been pretty clear with Billy."

"Yeah, but in Billy's world, there is only one right way to do something and that is his way. I have heard complaints about his tendency to micromanage his team and insist they do things 'the way they have always been done' and not to mess with success. Kind of the opposite of a continuous improvement mentality."

"Do you think his attitude is really going to derail our efforts or is it something that we can work around?"

"Should we have to work around him?" asked Josh. "Isn't he part of the senior leadership team? I pretty much think we should all be on the same team but I really don't trust the guy."

"He is so not a good team player. He almost never volunteers to help anyone else out. In fact, he almost seems to enjoy it when other folks are struggling," Josh vented. "Seriously, I cannot believe that he is not supporting our Kaizen efforts—the one Kaizen team that is focused on how to improve the work order process directly impacts his group!"

"Let me talk to Billy again," said Margaret. "I get that there are some issues, but I don't want to just dismiss such a skilled engineer. I really need for him to shape up—he's been on Performance Improvement Plans in the past and always seems to get just a little bit better before he reverts to form. I'll be firm with him that he needs to be supportive of the new initiatives and to watch his attitude with the rest of the team."

"Good luck with that." Josh shrugged. "I wouldn't be surprised if you have the same result. Remember Einstein!"

Two weeks later, Josh looked up from his monitor to see Mark from F&B (Food and Beverage) walking toward Josh's office, visibly upset.

"Josh, can we talk privately, please?"

"Mark, what's wrong?" Josh asked.

Mark closed the door and began pacing in frustration. "I seriously cannot work with that man anymore! Billy just jumped all over me about the mess left by that big group yesterday. A few things got broken and he ripped me a new one about the extra work for his guys. Then, to top it all off, he said that I may not understand the pressure that he was under because I spent so much time at the PRIDE festival over the weekend! Seriously, where does he get off saying that? I don't call him out for being at the monster truck rally!"

"Oh man, that is not okay," Josh groaned. "I'm so sorry that he offended you. Look, Margaret said she would talk to Billy about a few things, including how he comes across to others. Let me check with her and see how that went, and if I need to step in from an HR perspective, I will."

"This isn't the first time he's said things like that to me," said Mark. "I know he's been here a couple years longer than me, but that doesn't give him the right to treat me like an inferior. I won't just walk out on you, Josh, but if he doesn't change some things, pronto, I'll be looking elsewhere."

"Mark, I completely understand," said Josh. "I'll find out what's going on and do what I can to make this right."

Josh proceeded to talk Mark off the ledge and forty-five minutes later, Mark left, somewhat mollified.

I seriously need to talk to Margaret about how to approach this one later, Josh thought.

Just as Mark was leaving, Tiana swept into the office with a scowl on her face. "Josh, I just want to let you know that Billy was a total jerk to one of my new Front Desk agents, Pam. He had that poor thing in tears when he yelled at her about something that she had not even learned yet. Talk about not knowing how to give constructive feedback! He was downright offensive. You need to do something about him. I can't lose good staff because the head of another department chases them off." Before Josh could say a word in reply, the normally laid-back Tiana had turned and stormed out again.

Yikes, Josh thought. *This is even worse than I thought. Margaret and I have our meeting tomorrow morning, I'll definitely bring up this situation then.*

Just when he thought the day could not get worse, Jose from Engineering entered with a despondent look on his face.

"Josh, I'm here to give you my notice," said Jose quietly.

"Have a seat, please. What's this about, Jose? I thought you really liked it here and you have been doing so well. We don't want to lose you. Can you tell me more about what is going on?"

"I can't work for Billy any longer. I am so sorry to do this because I really think highly of you and of Margaret, but he says and does things that I just cannot tolerate. He has made fun of me being a Latino many times but he really stepped over the line today. When I pushed back on something, he told me to do—because I thought it was the wrong approach—he just told me to shut up unless I wanted someone to really start questioning my green card!" Josh closed his eyes in disbelief as Jose continued, "By the way, I was born in Texas and am a US citizen, for what it's worth! And there's more . . ."

Jose spoke for several minutes about Billy's lack of respect for the team, his inability to delegate or to let other people take accountability for anything, and his constant demeanor of disrespect. Josh listened, getting more and more frustrated. Clearly, Margaret's talks with Billy hadn't created any kind of lasting change in the chief engineer.

"Jose, this is serious stuff, and I want you to know I take it seriously," he said when the young engineer finally wound down. "If you really can't be here any longer, I understand. But we really do not want to lose you. You're one of our best engineers, and I know you have so much to give to Capitol House. Would you be willing to hold off for twenty-four hours so I can talk with Margaret and come up with a plan?"

Jose sighed. "Honestly, I'm not sure what you can do, but I'll give it a day. I do really like everything else about working at the hotel, but this is just too much."

"Thanks, Jose. I appreciate your trust."

After Jose left, Josh wasted no time hightailing it down to Margaret's office. His boss looked even more tired than usual as she looked up from yet another stack of reports. Her weariness quickly turned to frustration as Josh described the complaints that Mark, Tiana, and Jose had just given him.

"That darn Billy," she said. "I should have known he wasn't buying into the things we talked about. I thought things were getting better because he stopped making snide comments in staff meetings, but apparently, I was wrong. What are we going to do? I guess I'll write him up for a Performance Improvement Plan again, but where do I even start? There are so many problems to pick from, and every one he's already heard about at least once!"

Josh shook his head firmly. "Margaret, we have just spent a significant amount of time and energy defining our values and articulating what kind of culture we want to have. Billy is clearly not demonstrating those values and pretty much never has during his tenure. He may be a case of someone who just does not fit within our culture. Despite his technical skills, his manner and behavior are preventing us from solidifying our culture and making it mean something. Plus, we've now gotten to a point where if we keep Billy, we lose at least two other people who really DO fit with the culture we want—Mark and Jose. I think we need to walk the talk and he just needs to go—no PIP this time—just let him go. He is not going to change and we will not be successful at building a strong culture while he is here. He is just a bad apple."

Margaret took a deep breath, thinking for a long moment before looking back up at Josh. "You know, I think you are right. No PIP is going to ever change what needs to be different with Billy. I'll be sad to lose a chief engineer of his experience, but we can't torpedo the rest of the hotel staff just for one person. I think we just need to invite him to go be happy elsewhere."

Josh gave a small sigh of relief. "I'm glad we agree on that. Let's work on our talking points and plan of attack so we can talk to him later today. After that, we'll circle back with Jose and the others."

The Solution

While the example of Billy, the Chief Engineer, may seem a bit extreme, we've all dealt with employees whose performance or behavior wasn't what it needed to be—especially when changes in culture start to happen. In this chapter, we'll look at how to handle these situations—and the people in them.

The phrase "performance management" can send chills down the spines of many leaders. But it doesn't have to. If a leader or manager is doing an effective job of providing constructive feedback and delegating appropriately, it should not be hard to either keep people on track or to solve problems. It takes focus and deliberate action (like most other aspects of leadership), but once you learn the skills, it is not hard.

CONSTRUCTIVE FEEDBACK

Let's start with feedback—why do we give it? The purpose of feedback is to provide constructive, descriptive information that enables the person to either:

- MAINTAIN a positive behavior (continue)

- ENHANCE to a higher level (do even more or build on)

- CHANGE a negative or ineffective behavior (stop or do differently)

The key here is the word *constructive*. The foundation of giving good constructive feedback is trust in the relationship, so that the receiver knows the input is coming from a place of helpfulness. The definition of constructive is important.

Constructive means helpful, beneficial, or developmental; designed to improve and grow something rather than to destroy or detract from it.

In other words, constructive feedback is meant to help the other person continue good performance or to do better. It is not about venting or making the *speaker* feel better. It is clear that giving constructive feedback makes many people quite uncomfortable as they believe that it can lead to conflict—which most people wish to avoid like the plague. However, by learning to effectively give constructive feedback, managers can actually give a powerful gift to the other person.

Self-awareness is the first step in professional development. Managers can and should provide input to employees on what might otherwise be a career show-stopper. The ability to do this well is not a talent—it is skill and can be learned. The following is a really useful model for creating and delivering feedback with four steps—the DESC model.

D — Describe the behavior

E — Express why it matters

S — Seek or specify a solution

C — Collaborate to agree on a path forward

Here is an example of how this could work. Imagine Margaret is giving feedback to Billy about his attitude and lack of support for the team efforts.

Describe **D**	The situation, the problem, the behavior (WHAT) Focus on the problem, not the person Use "I" messages; avoid starting with "You" Include example(s), documentation	Bill, I need to talk to you about some behavior that I have observed in our team planning meetings. I've noticed you seem skeptical of our work, have been critical of our work, are making sarcastic comments, and have not volunteered for any of the follow-up projects.
Express **E**	The impact or importance (WHY) Customer Team/department Individual	This behavior is a problem for me and the rest of the team as it undermines our work and demonstrates a lack of respect. As a result, people don't trust that you will help implement the changes.
Seek/ **Specify** **S**	Alternative solutions/options to minimize impact and ensure future success. Collaborate rather than impose solutions (HOW) Greater ownership of the action plan 95% "seek" mutually agreeable solution 5% "specify" action for severe situations	What can we do to help you feel better about our work so you are comfortable getting on board and supporting the team? How would you suggest that we change the process or what should we do instead to move forward? *(mutual discussion here)*

Collaborate **C**	A closing statement about how the solution will affect the future. Lead with positive; follow up with negative 95% positive; 5% negative Avoid idle threats; follow through	So, you agree that you will suggest an alternative every time that you object to a group idea and that you will not lead with sarcasm any longer. I think that will really help our management team to start to jell more effectively so that we can drive positive change.

Some additional feedback guidelines include:

Provide *specific* examples	Avoid generic statements that could apply to *anyone*. The more concrete and specific, the bettter.
Focus on behaviors, not attitude	Performance behaviors can change; although attitude influences behavior, it is the behavior change that we want in the workplace.
Choose *words* carefully that won't provoke emotions and defensiveness	Making off-hand remarks, cynical comments, or using hot-button words stalls behavior change and fails to create performance improvement.
Do not analyze intent or motivation	Refrain from adding, "and I think you are doing this because…" It is worth considering what *might* be contributing to the problem behavior but analyzing the person's intent is not part of the problem-solving process. Few adults want to be analyzed by armchair psychologists. Any negative comments will likely be denied or defended— neither helpful to improving performance.
Avoid *absolutes* (always, never)	*"You're never on time to meetings, you always dominate the meetings."* These are fighting words. People will generally focus on finding exceptions to such generalizations.

Timely feedback is more meaningful and effective	Keep feedback close to the event rather than weeks or months after (for both positive and corrective feedback). It is perceived as more genuine and accurate.
Praise in public; correct in private	Err on the side of public recognition of positive contributions, even though some personalities prefer only low-key, one-on-one or written praise. Corrective feedback is *not* to be done in a public setting (staff meetings, corridors, outside office cubicles, etc.).
Avoid *broadcast* feedback	Messages given to an entire group rather than to the individuals who deserve the feedback offend or punish those who don't deserve the feedback. At the same time, the message tends not to be heard or acted upon by those who need the feedback the most. Managers who don't step up to deliver tough messages to individuals lose credibility and respect from their work group. Even positive feedback broadcast to a group ought to have individual contributions recognized one-on-one.

Let's talk for a minute about the feedback needs and preferences of the new generation in the workplace. Many studies have indicated that millennials and gen-z employees are more comfortable getting or giving feedback electronically than face-to-face. On one hand, hotel managers can accommodate this by applying their constructive feedback skills to electronic or email communications with the employees. On the other hand, since interpersonal effectiveness is generally a development need for many younger workers, managers can model the skills of effectively giving direct and constructive feedback, listening, and coaching in regular one-on-one coaching meetings. In our experience, we have seen millennials respond pretty positively to this kind of feedback, given frequently and with constructive intent.

PERFORMANCE CORRECTION

Sometimes, despite our best efforts, the performance of an employee is not acceptable. Once the employee has been coached (using our constructive feedback model) but the results are not happening, we may need to move to the next step in performance correction.

Most organizations utilize a progressive disciplinary process, with the caveat that it can be bypassed depending upon the unique circumstances of each situation. There are generally three things that managers should attempt to accomplish with a Performance Improvement Plan (PIP):

1. First and foremost, the goal of performance correction is to correct performance that is not acceptable. It is intended to change the performance so that it is no longer a problem.

2. A secondary goal is to ensure that the employee is treated fairly and that the organization has indeed provided clear direction about performance expectations, has given adequate tools and support, and generally support an environment in which employees can succeed.

3. Finally, the grim reality of employment litigation means that a third goal of a performance correction process is to

build a file and develop proper documentation in the event that an individual's employment with the company would need to be terminated. A well-written PIP can greatly support the termination decision and document how we got there.

However, *before* jumping to a PIP, we recommend that a manager take a few minutes to step back and try to figure out what is happening. What could be the root cause of the employee's behavior or insufficient performance? Below is a list of some good questions to ask yourself—most of which will be easy to answer and will not require much, if any, investigation. This exercise is more about self-reflection to ensure that the problem is not the manager but is indeed the employee.

- Is the employee aware of the performance expectations? Do they know what you want them to do?

- Does the employee have the skill and/or ability to perform?

- Has the training been sufficient? Does the employee know *how* to do the job?

- Does the employee have the necessary tools/equipment?

- Has the behavior been addressed previously? If so, how long ago?

- How long has the employee been with the hotel?

- Have there been other, related performance problems?

- Is there a motivation problem with the employee?

- Could there be personal problems/issues that are negatively impacting the employee's ability to perform?

The key to determining these root causes is to **ASK** and **LISTEN**. In some cases, you can ask the employee directly. In others, you may want to ask another supervisor, the team lead, or even another employee. Don't make assumptions. The answers to these types of questions will allow the supervisor to formulate an approach that is appropriate to the situation.

If it is appropriate to move to a PIP, then the PIP should be written in a way that provides documented feedback to the employee about what the problem is and what needs to change. The PIP should generally lay out a timeline for improvement and include check-ins to evaluate progress (see example at the end of the book). It should also address possible consequences if the behavior is not corrected. Ideally, the employee will make the needed changes and successfully pass out of the PIP process.

One cautionary note here: in our experience, the PIP process too often falls apart when managers neglect the follow up with the employee. Too much time passes and the employee can rightfully (and possibly erroneously) start to think that no news is good news and that all is now fine. When the manager finally gets around to following up, if the behavior is still not acceptable, it may be difficult to move to the next level or to termination because there has been no additional feedback or assistance in how to improve. In some instances, you may end up starting all over. Regular documented follow-up is essential for a good PIP process.

A word about documentation here: Just do it. Supervisory documentation—of both the good and the bad performance—on each employee can make a manager's job so much easier. Take notes on a regular basis—in any format that you like—paper or electronic. An important suggestion is to always date the notes so that you can recreate a timeline if needed.

WHY IS DOCUMENTATION SO IMPORTANT?

- Important in order to give factual, accurate feedback

- Helps to spot trends and patterns

- Will be necessary evidence in case of a lawsuit or unemployment claim.

There are *two types of documentation* that are essential in managing marginal performance.

1. **Documentation for your files.** This will provide you with the necessary background facts and details needed to effectively manage this performance problem.

   Use your best judgment in determining when and how to document performance issues. For example, it is a good idea to jot notes of attendance problems for your employees. It may not be appropriate to give out a written warning at this time.

   Managers should document all verbal coaching that they discuss with employees. This does not need to be given to the employee. Create and maintain a supervisor file on each of your employees.

   It is possible to over-document. Too much documentation could undermine the credibility of the manager, or make it look like a particular employee has been "targeted." Make sure you document in a relatively equal manner. Don't just document one employee's behavior and not do the same for the other employees.

2. **Documentation to be given to the employee.** This is a way to communicate your expectations, problems, etc.

with the employee. These are the "PIPS" or "warnings" to the employee.

Guidelines for good performance documentation include:

- ✓ Explain both the problem and the impact that it causes. Why is this a concern?

- ✓ Avoid "jargon" that can be misunderstood.

- ✓ Show notice and that an employee has been given the opportunity to change.

- ✓ Give a copy of the document to the employee.

- ✓ Date and sign the document.

- ✓ Have the employee sign an acknowledgment, if possible.

- ✓ Follow the company rules—abide by existing policies, contracts, etc.

- ✓ Beware of precedent—be consistent.

- ✓ Take into consideration other legal "protections"— FMLA, ADA, etc.

- ✓ Be factual—tell the story. Tell the truth.

- ✓ Describe behaviors—not "attitudes."

- ✓ Avoid conclusions.

- ✓ Avoid adjectives and adverbs.

- ✓ Avoid labels.

- ✓ Explain the consequences.

EMPLOYEE TERMINATION

Generally, we regard turnover as something to be managed and minimized, if possible. This section of our book illustrates that not all turnover is bad turnover. There are times when, like in our story, it is best to make the difficult decision to move on from an employee. This can be because the employee just is not a good fit with your culture—and never will be. It can happen when there is a mismatch of skills between the employee and the needs of a job. It can happen when an employee has other priorities and the job is not a good fit. Sometimes, if things have changed in the hotel and the employee completely resists the change, it may no longer the right match. As long as the termination decisions are for legitimate, non-discriminatory reasons, the best option may be to choose to move on and like Margaret did, "invite those employees to go be happy elsewhere!"

CHAPTER FIVE

R.E.S.P.E.C.T!

The Story

Josh stopped to catch his breath as he reflected back on the past few weeks. With Billy's departure, they not only had to cover his duties on an interim basis, but there was a lot of damage control needed within the team. More than Josh had expected. He wearily dropped into the guest chair in Margaret's office.

"I just facilitated an employee meeting with the remaining employees in the Engineering and Maintenance Department. Wow, did they unload on me! Things with Billy were even worse than we thought."

"That really makes me feel like an idiot for not acting sooner," Margaret said. "I guess that 'one bad apple' adage has some validity. Is there anything else that we can do to let the team know that we care and that we value them and what they do?"

"Well, for sure we need to implement some respectful workplace training—and make it required for anyone in a leadership or supervisory role. Billy's biases were way too evident in how he treated the employees. Also, I think we need to be much more deliberate in celebrating the unique differences among our employees—we need to think more about how to do that."

Margaret took a deep breath. "You know, you've actually caused me to think. Not just for this position, but I'm thinking you're on to something. I think before we do any training, we need to first work on developing and implementing a real and defined 'culture of respect' model that we can roll out through the entire hotel. Every department can benefit. Remember the issues we had in Housekeeping? I think we need to be much clearer about what we mean when we say that we will treat each other with respect. Let's add that to the agenda at the next management team meeting."

"And now that Billy is gone, we need to think more about what kind of person we want to fill the chief engineer role," Josh said.

"What do you mean what kind of person? A qualified one," Margaret replied. "We need to focus on strong hotel-based engineering and maintenance experience. Previous people and project management experience is critical too. We need to get that job posted right away."

Disappointed by her response, Josh decided to count to ten before responding. "Wait a minute, we need more than that. Think about all the work we have done with defining our culture and our values. The straw that broke the camel's back with Billy was when we realized that he would never be a good fit with our culture. Remember how he reacted to other team members? We need to do a better job of determining a culture fit with our next leader."

Margaret nodded. "You're right, we do need to focus on that as well. Just so we can find both!"

"There's more. I spent a lot of time talking Billy's employees off the ledge when he was disrespectful to them. Many of his employees were Latino and he was sometimes downright offensive to them. Not to mention how awful he was with Mark. We need to make sure the new chief engineer supports diversity and treats everyone with respect—not just you. We have a lot of work to do here in better understanding and responding to the individual differences of our employees."

"You're right. But that's a lot to find in one person. Are you sure we can do it?"

"It may not be easy but we do need to focus on finding a good, all-around fit. If we have to give on anything, we may have to back off on having identical hotel engineer experience and find someone with the soft skills. We can teach the nuances of hotels, but we can't teach character!"

"I think I get what you are saying—I'm not entirely sure that I agree," Margaret replied. "But I do know that we can't have someone who is as disrespectful as Billy was—he was like a cancer to the morale of the team. I guess what I'm really saying is—let's not let 'great get in the way of good.' We'll never find a person that matches our every desire."

"That's a fair point," Josh said. "Let's do this. Let's go through all the qualifications we need this person to have. Some are no-brainers, things they gotta' have. HVAC Certification, for example. Then, there are the soft skills—people management, training, coaching, etc. Then, we'll decide how much weight to put on each skill. Kind of like building a GSS score on each candidate. Who will most closely match our 'perfect fit.' And I'm listening. I got your point about not letting 'great get in the way of good.' There are a lot of good candidates out there. We just need to find the one that's the best fit for us."

Margaret nodded. "That would accomplish a number of things. First, it would help us know who most closely matches our needs and wants, then it would show us that most candidates are not perfect, but there are a lot of good ones out there. And finally, I'm thinking it will actually improve our hiring process and ultimately our GSS scores. Because we 'grade' each candidate in a way that meaningfully and truly ties their skill sets directly back to the needs of the hotel.

"We've worked way too hard on our culture to allow a few people to disrupt that. We saw with Billy what a huge impact just one bad apple can have. It's critical that we don't make that same mistake in hiring his successor."

The Solution

Everyone wants to (and deserves to) work in a place where they are treated fairly and with respect.

On the surface, the phrase "Respectful Workplace" seems like it should be easy to achieve. In real life and in our hotels, it takes a lot more than saying it to make it reality. In order to create and foster this, we must first clearly understand the actual definition.

A respectful workplace is one where all team members are treated fairly; differences are acknowledged, respected, and valued; communication is open and civil; conflict is addressed early; and there is a culture of empowerment and cooperation. Most important, it is a place where all employees feel safe in being who they are.

Hotels are often diverse workplaces—which is what helps to make them so special. There is a richness to the culture as a result of the wide range of backgrounds and personalities of the employees. However, leaders must be aware that the downside of significant diversity in the workplace is an increased likelihood for misunderstandings.

It is easy to talk about supporting Diversity and Inclusion (D & I) efforts, but we've noticed that managers have a tendency to narrowly define this concept. We are not just talking about major cultural differences or gender or age. We mean overall diversity of thought, experience, and background. The richness of different ideas can bring great value to our hotels—if we recognize and support it.

Some ways to help establish and support a respectful workplace include:

- **Training**—Ensure that all employees are clear about what is acceptable in the workplace, and what is not is acceptable. Provide training about what to do (and not do) in the hotel environment. As we discussed earlier, a code of conduct can be helpful.

- **Consistent, timely feedback and course corrections**—It is not uncommon to learn that an employee's behaviors are offensive to someone, yet the issue has not been addressed with that employee. Providing feedback quickly permits a change in behavior and may stave off any future issues. Being comfortable with any cultural or style differences can help managers be more effective.

- **It starts at the top**—If managers are not firm with their expectations for themselves and for others, small issues and concerns begin to creep in, which can then open the door to more concerning behavior. By maintaining professional standards in the hotel, this limits the chances of creating an unacceptable workplace setting.

- **The Bystander Effect**—If you see something, say something. Make it clear that every employee contributes to a respectful work culture, and if they see or hear something that may be offensive or disrespectful, it is up to that employee to do something. Say something. Follow up. Talk to a manager. Whatever it takes—ignoring it and hoping the problem will go away is not ok.

- **Establishing clear procedures for reporting these types of behavior**—This is critical to ensuring that any problems that may arise are handled swiftly, fairly, and firmly. Make sure there are multiple avenues for employees to bring forward complaints so at least one option feels safe for them.

When participating in diversity and respect conversations with some hotel leaders, we often hear the statement: "we follow the Golden Rule—treat others the way in which we would like to be treated." While this is a good first step in creating a respectful workplace, it doesn't take into consideration individual differences. We recommend following the "platinum rule"—treat others the way in which *they* wish to be treated.

If your hotel has a large population of a particular culture or ethnicity, it makes sense for you as the leader to learn a bit more about some of the characteristics and norms of that group so that you can effectively adjust your leadership style. For example, in some Asian cultures, it is considered disrespectful to challenge one's elders. If your hotel has many Asian employees, and you promote a younger worker to a team lead role with older employees, you may need to provide additional coaching and assistance in how to give work direction, provide feedback, and hold them accountable. Otherwise, the team lead may not be able to succeed in this assignment.

LET'S TALK GENERATIONS

One subset of differences in the workplace is the generational diversity that we see in our hotels. Much has been written about the unique needs and preferences of the millennials in particular (those born roughly between 1980 and 2000). Earlier in our careers, we received training on how very different these millennials are, only to find out that the differences between millennials and the previous generations are no more profound than the differences that history has noted in the past every time a new generation comes of age.

We both wonder at the frustration that we often hear when older hotel managers are venting about the millennials. Yes, change requires flexibility, but it also can bring growth. Just as Margaret is benefiting from creating a respectful working relationship with Josh in our story, so hotel managers can learn to see the different approaches millennials bring to work as assets, not liabilities. Millennials tend to be more tech savvy, more connected, more socially aware, and more vocal about what they need than are their older counterparts. These traits can help your hotel be more up-to-date, stay more diverse, give more immediate and personal customer service, and solve problems more quickly—if you let them. Continuous learning, career growth, recognition, and flexibility are key requirements for millennials in the workplace—often of equal or even greater importance than salary levels. Experienced hotel leaders need to be sure that they are keeping up with these changing expectations. We need to understand that what a "good culture" looks like to our millennial employees may be quite different from what it means to our baby boomers, and be prepared to build that culture for them rather than expecting them to conform to how things have been for the last thirty years.

Having said that, millennials do have some unique (and at times, frustrating—to other generations) characteristics and expectations of the workplace. The first is that they often demonstrate little regard for age and wisdom. They are not typically interested in "paying their dues" and don't always appreciate those who have done so. This may be the crux of much of the tension between baby boomers and millennials—neither generation wants to feel discounted and disrespected by the other.

Millennials want managers and leaders who focus more on *what* they do rather than *how* they accomplish their work. They are much less inclined to just blindly follow directions, and often require some context and an understanding of why a process is important before they will adhere to it. This can be another source of frustration for longer-term leaders who want employees to "do it because I told you to." Command and control does not work with this generation. They will respect their leaders more for their abilities than for their job titles.

Your millennial employees want their ideas to be heard and to feel that they are making significant contributions. The Lean continuous improvement process that we have discussed is a good way to involve them in finding new solutions and sourcing new ideas; and the incorporation of millennials within the process may increase credibility and, ultimately, buy in.

Interestingly, more flexibility in work is a common refrain that we are hearing from *all* generations (even though it's usually seen as a millennial desire). We can give the millennials credit for bringing this issue into the spotlight, but surveys have found that every generation in the workplace—from baby boomers who may be winding down in their careers, to Gen Xers who want to work remotely, to millennials who want time for their other interests—all would like to see more flexibility at work. Smart leaders will not reject this preference out of hand but will think hard about ways to provide flexibility when possible in a hotel.

As the following visual illustrates, there are many areas of common interest among the generations in your work environment. Our experience has been that it pays to highlight the similarities within your team and then manage the differences as much as possible.

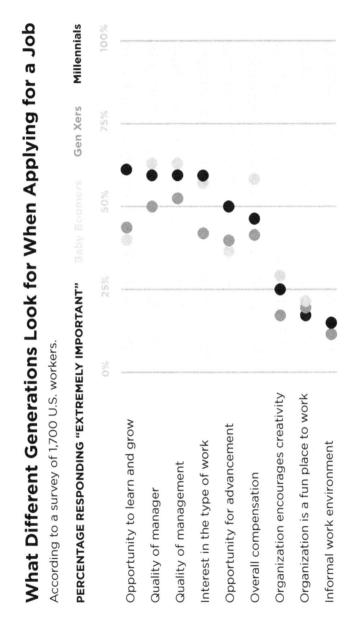

What Different Generations Look for When Applying for a Job

According to a survey of 1,700 U.S. workers.

PERCENTAGE RESPONDING "EXTREMELY IMPORTANT"

Brandon Rigoni and Amy Adkins, "What Millennials Want from a New Job," Harvard Business Review, May 11, 2016, https://hbr.org/2016/05/what-millennials-want-from-a-new-job.

ME TOO (#METOO)

Last, we need to talk about gender diversity and respectful workplaces with both men and women. As all too many recent cases and news stories illustrate, US workplaces are still experiencing a major problem in how they treat women on the job. The American Psychological Association estimates that 60 percent of women voters have been subjected to sexual harassment at some point in their careers. That is more than half of all women in the workplace![4] This lack of respect for women in the workplace can happen in any type of organization—hotels are no exception.

Regardless of the intention of the person doing the behavior, if the impact is that someone else feels uncomfortable, it needs to stop. This includes people who like to hug and kiss or call folks "honey," or people who act like bullies and make intimidating statements, jokes, or teasing. If it makes someone feel disrespected, it has to stop.

This #MeToo movement is working to erase any shame and embarrassment associated with being a victim of this kind of behavior. This movement has really shined a spotlight on creating and supporting a culture of respect with zero tolerance for harassing behavior.

As hotel leaders, we must value the unique perspectives that women bring to the workplace *and* ensure that we create and support an environment that does not support any type of harassment—sexual or otherwise. It is our job as leaders to provide a safe work environment that is free from harassment and disrespectful behavior.

We have included a short quiz about respectful workplace in the resource section at the back of the book (5.1) that can be used for Respectful Workplace Training.

---

4   Brendan L. Smith, "What it really takes to stop sexual harassment," *Monitor on Psychology* 49, no. 2 (February 2018): 36, https://www.apa.org/monitor/2018/02/sexual-harassment.aspx.

CHAPTER 6

"THE SHIFT BEGINS"

The Story

Margaret walked into Josh's office and noticed a look of despair on his face. "Don't tell me," she said. "Not another Billy situation?"

"No, thank God. But this is just as bad in a completely different way. We're hemorrhaging workers."

"You mean they're just leaving?"

"Yup. Maria from Housekeeping—she's the fourth one this week. That new hotel down the street is poaching from us big time. They are offering a higher starting rate with six-month reviews and raises, flexible shifts, and benefits for an employee's partner or spouse. I wish we could look at offering some of that stuff! If we can't be competitive enough to keep our workers, none of the rest of this stuff will matter."

Margaret closed his door and sat down. "You know what, Josh, I think I've been wrong. I was just sitting in my office and started thinking about that old phrase by Einstein you told me about."

Josh laughed, "You mean his definition of insanity? *Doing the same thing over and over and expecting different results?*"

"That's the one. Everything about managing people seems to be changing and I don't really know what to do to change the way I have operated for years. Clearly, our high turnover is a symptom of some of the other issues that we have started to address. I realize that this new generation of workers is looking for different things from a job and a workplace than what I did when I was younger. I think we are making some progress with all of our efforts on culture and diversity, but I've never had turnover like this before. People are even leaving us to go to hotels that are not as nice or as well run as this. And it's so hard to find replacements in this tight labor market. Some days, I wonder if I should just give up and retire."

Josh looked startled. "Now that doesn't sound like you, Margaret. From what I know about you, you have never been a quitter! Things are bad now but we can get through this."

"Yes, if we can figure out how to work together better, maybe we will have a chance." She put up her hand to stop Josh from responding. "Let me finish before you say anything. I need to own this. I've started to listen to some of your ideas but I really haven't embraced the changes that you have been talking about, or, in truth, accepted you as my partner. I haven't been 'all in' on your ideas and I think I owe you an apology for that."

Josh's mouth fell open. Had he really heard that? Finally, he said, "Margaret, you do know that I'm on your side, right? You can trust me to do what I can to help."

Margaret actually seemed to have tears in her eyes. "Oh, trust. That is such a big word and one that I am not very good at. I do realize that I can't do it all myself, I need to trust you and other folks to help get us out of this mess. But in the past few months, you have given me every reason to trust you and I haven't let my guard down. That's going to change!"

"You know," Josh said, "I agree with you but it's not a one-way street. There have been times where I should have respected your experience and depth of knowledge but I kept thinking that I knew a better way. In truth, the better way is probably us together and neither you or me individually."

Margaret laughed. "Is this our Kum Ba Yah moment?"

"Boy, that brings me back to Boy Scout Camp! Yeah, it probably is our moment. You know, it's like Kimbr reminded us a while back: you care about Capitol House and I care about Capitol House. If the two of us could stay on the same page, we could really turn things around. This is our chance."

Both sighed deeply. Then Margaret said, "This retention thing, it's not just about money is it?"

"No, not entirely. Money is important, but I think that is just the tip of the iceberg. If people don't feel they are paid fairly, not much else matters. But it's only one of a number of factors, as we see with the new hotel offering other benefits we don't. But I don't just want to start doing what another hotel is doing, because they aren't Capitol House. Frankly, I think we need to stop guessing at what those factors are, start asking our workers more questions and really listening to their responses." Josh hesitated, then continued when he saw he had Margaret's full attention. "I know I have brought up this idea before and you were pretty cool to it—"

Margaret interrupted, "You really mean that I totally shot you down! That was not fair and I am sorry about that."

"It's alright," said Josh. "We're moving forward now, that's the important thing. Anyway, maybe instead of telling the employees what we are offering, we need to let them tell us what we should be doing. We talked earlier about improving our employees' overall experience in the hotel. We've made some good changes so far—from making the move to replace Billy to involving our employees in the Lean Kaizen process to help make good change in establishing what kind of culture we want to have. However, I'm not real sure that either you or I can accurately guess what a great employee experience looks like for each of our employees. Let's consider an employee engagement survey. It wouldn't be difficult to do and will most likely give us some great insights. At the very least, we get credit for asking for their input."

Margaret nodded. "An engagement survey might be a good project for the management team to tackle—it may help everyone feel more like they own part of the issues instead of assuming it's all on me! Let's suggest it at our meeting next week. Can you bring in some samples to start the conversation?"

"Absolutely. Leave it to me. Now, as long as we are talking it, let me take this one step further. I think we need to go beyond the hotel culture and create an actual employee experience."

Margaret stopped writing. "An employee experience? You tried to tell me about that before but I confess, I didn't really pay that much attention. Tell me more."

"Well," Josh took a deep breath. It's like taking the idea of Customer Experience and translating it into how we deal with our employees—providing the EX. I learned a lot about it at the HR conference I went to a couple months back. The employee experience, or EX, is the total experience an employee has from the moment they join our team until the moment they leave it. And it's a lot like a hotel's culture—we as the hotel managers can shape or design the EX, or not, but every employee's going to have one either way. So it makes a lot of sense to design one rather than let it happen on its own."

Margaret nodded thoughtfully. "I could see that. And having a purposeful EX helps mitigate turnover, right?"

"Exactly!" said Josh. "When employees have a positive experience, they want to stay—so by asking them what makes an experience positive, we put ourselves in a better position to give them those things, or at least as much of them as is workable. We can start with the results of the employee engagement surveys, and I'll do some research into best practices to supplement those. How does that sound?"

"Sounds like a plan to me," said Margaret. "I'll look forward to seeing what you come up with—and I really mean that this time!"

The Solution

In 2016, the US Bureau of Labor Statistics documented 72.9 percent annualized employee turnover rate in the hospitality industry. That is more than 6 percent of our hotel teams departing every month![5] This is clearly a challenge for our entire industry—and is much higher than in other sectors. However, we do know from experience that focused attention on culture and the employee experience CAN bring that turnover number down.

The employee experience is all about meeting or exceeding our employees' expectations throughout their entire career with your hotel. When an organization is experiencing high levels of unwanted turnover, it is a clear sign that all is not as it should be. Leaders need to understand that something is wrong within the employee experience and that it is time for a change.

---

5   "Hospitality employee turnover rate edged higher in 2016," National Restaurant Association, March 16, 2017, https://www.restaurant.org/News-Research/News/Hospitality-employee-turnover-rate-edged-higher-in.

Research shows that a focus on EX pays off. Specifically, *The Employee Experience Advantage* by Jacob Morgan showed evidence that organizations that invest most heavily in EX were:

- Included 11.5 times as often in Glassdoor's Best Places to Work

- Listed 4.4 times as often in LinkedIn's list of North America's Most In-Demand Employers

- Listed 28 times more often among Fast Company's Most Innovative Companies

- Listed 2.1 times as often on the Forbes list of the World's Most Innovative Companies

- Found twice as often in the American Customer Satisfaction Index[6]

Most importantly, Morgan noted that that "experiential organizations had more than four times the average profit and more than two times the average revenue. They were also almost 25 percent smaller, which suggests higher levels of productivity and innovation."

Morgan's research clearly supports the notion that a focus on the employee experience leads to satisfied and engaged employees, which makes them perform at a higher level, which, in turn, enhances the guest experience and ultimately will demonstrate a positive impact on the bottom line. Happy employees lead to happy guests, which leads to a happy GM with great bottom-line results.

Clearly, a focus on the entire employee experience will take time and effort, but the results seem to be worth it.

---

6   Jacob Morgan, *The Employee Experience Advantage: How to Win the War for Talent by Giving Employees the Workspaces they Want, the Tools they Need, and a Culture They Can Celebrate* (Hoboken: Wiley, 2017).

Yes, the world has changed and our hotel teams have changed. If we wish to continue to run an outstanding hotel, then we must have outstanding teams.

In this chapter, we investigate a few strategies for doing things differently in order to enhance employee retention.

TRUST

One of the first elements associated with effectively retaining employees is to develop and support a trusting relationship between leaders and employees. We touched on some key elements needed to build a strong employee culture in Chapter 2, but trust goes even deeper than that.

You have likely heard the expression, "Employees don't quit companies, they quit their managers." Numerous studies about why people quit their jobs indicate that distrust or dislike of (or by) the direct manager was paramount.

Just like our story illustrated, trust is a necessary component of every great organization and employee experience. We have both witnessed the pervasive problems that become systemic within an organization where people don't trust each other. It is up to the hotel leaders to establish, support, and model trust in the workplace.

This starts with "assuming positive intent" for other people's actions—don't jump to the conclusion that they're just trying to make your life miserable. Trust that they had a good reason for their actions and try to understand before responding.

A lack of trust can cost a hotel significant time and money—whether it shows up as a people issue, a sales concern, or another problem. David Horsager, chief executive officer of Trust Edge Leadership Institute, has done some interesting work around how to build a trusting work environment. Much of it starts with good leadership.

Horsager's research identifies eight critical qualities of effective and trusted leaders. They are:

1. **Clarity.** "People trust the clear and they distrust the ambiguous." This is why it is important for managers to be absolutely clear about their vision and their expectations. Let your employees know what you want. What makes our hotel unique and how do you contribute to that vision? It will resonate more clearly with your employees when you say that our hotel will be known for outstanding customer service—that every guest interaction will exceed expectations. This makes it clear what you expect of every employee.

2. **Compassion.** Leaders who demonstrate that they care about others will inspire trust. Employees will want to follow this type of leader. Truly empathizing with the myriad of challenges facing our employees and helping them figure out how to address these issues will not only help the employee, but will also build an environment of trust and loyalty. By showing some heart, hotel leaders will become someone that most employees want to work for.

3. **Character.** This means doing the right thing—even when no one is looking. Do what is right rather than what is easy. As a hotel leader, it is up to you to step up and make the right decisions within the hotel. Your integrity will help your employees trust that you will always do the right thing. You are not going to say one thing and do another.

4. **Competency.** Employees will trust a manager who stays fresh, relevant, and capable. You don't need to be the best at every task, but you do need to be capable. If there

are aspects of the hotel operations that are new to you, then admit that and be open to learning. This helps to demonstrate that it is important to be good at your job, and that we all can keep learning and improving.

5. **Commitment.** If a manager "has the back" of their employees, then their employees will in turn support the leader. Employees are more likely to make informed decisions and take reasonable risks in order to excel in their jobs if they know that the leader will support their efforts.

6. **Connection.** Effective managers will cultivate strong relationships at work. Ask questions and really listen. Find common ground with those of different backgrounds. Getting to know your employees as people is an important first step in developing trust. When you see them as people with full lives—families, interests, and problems—it is easier to connect to, empathize with, and trust each other.

7. **Contribution.** Make a difference and produce results. Employees will not trust if the manager is not competent and impactful. We have seen huge culture differences between hotels—all based on the behavior of the general manager. In the hotel where the GM rarely pokes his head out of his office, it was rare that any of the other employees ever went above and beyond for the customers. In contrast, the hotel in which the GM walked around the entire hotel and greeted every employee she saw each morning was always in the top tier for overall performance.

8. **Consistency.** What we do all the time shapes what other expect of us. If leaders are consistent in their behavior, then employees will know what to expect and trust what they

see. What you see is what you get. Employees don't want to "guess" about your reaction to a situation. They will react better (and stress less) when they are comfortable with how the leader is likely to react. This reassurance will bring out the best in your employees and provide them with a safe environment in which to make their best decisions.[7]

LISTENING

As managers, we often listen to respond, rather than listening to understand. Never is this more important than when focusing on associate retention.

The Lean Kaizen process is one example of the importance of listening—in a Kaizen process, your job is to listen to *everyone*. If we honestly want to know what will encourage our employees to stay longer, engage more, service our guests better, and ultimately show a greater ROI, then the answer is simple: Ask them and act on the responses. Find out what will make your employees excited to be at work and try to provide those things to enhance their experience.

ENGAGEMENT SURVEYS

Periodic engagement surveys have been used in many hotels for years. They can be an effective way to listen to employee feedback, to take the pulse of the organizations, and to point leaders in the right direction about what needs to change. The key to success is to be sure that you as the hotel leader acknowledge the input, communicate the results of the survey, and then act. You don't need to implement every single idea that comes from the survey—however, you need to hear

---

7   David Horsager, "The 8 Pillars of Trust that Will Make or Break Your Business," Interview by Donald Miller, 2017, http://buildingastorybrand.com/episode-52.

the feedback, determine the importance of each idea, identify the priorities, and define a plan to address the key ideas. No matter how you approach it—you must do something with the input. To ask and do nothing is far worse than not asking at all.

While, historically, hotels and other organizations have done lengthy, detailed employee engagement surveys every six or twelve months, we suggest using shorter, more frequent "pulse" surveys instead. This practice allows you to be more focused, nimbler, and able to respond in real time to concerns—before they go on for too long or escalate.

For example, you may design a simple survey tool to be given quarterly in order to "take the pulse" of the employees on different areas of their experience. A pulse survey will have no more than six to ten questions, with a different focus every quarter. The first quarter can be around culture and communication; the second around career development and training; the third around pay and benefits; and the fourth around leadership and company direction. After you gather the input from the surveys, convene a cross-functional team that is charged with understanding and developing strategies to address some of the key concerns that come out of the surveys. If a cross-section of the employees is charged with creating the solutions, then they will likely have a greater sense of buy-in to the ideas. This team is also accountable for communication back to the employees. (You'll notice that this team process works very similarly to a Kaizen team—this is not a coincidence!)

There are examples of some pulse survey questions in Resources & Samples, section 5.1.

There are many new software tools to support this kind of survey—as well continuous feedback and recognition. In the absence of a software budget, a short SurveyMonkey survey is better than nothing. We do realize that technology can still be a challenge for some hotel employees. In that case, paper copies done at one of the daily huddle meetings can be just as beneficial. Bring cookies along for anyone who completes the survey (and even for those who don't).

TWO-WAY MEETINGS

One common roadblock to getting honest, reliable feedback from your employees is that workers of all levels often struggle to give open feedback to (or in front of) their immediate supervisors. This may be simple nervousness or fear of "doing it wrong," but it may also include a very logical reluctance to give feedback on the supervisors themselves and risk harming that working relationship. Everyone may love complaining about their boss, but no one wants to actually tell the boss he has a problem.

To combat this tendency, a very effective way of listening to your employees is to create a process for systematic, deliberate meetings between selected employees and senior leaders *without the employee's direct supervisor present.* (In other words, instead of meeting with your boss, you'd meet with *their* boss.) For example, the GM (and possibly the HRD) will have lunch and talk with a selected number of housekeepers without the Housekeeping Managers/Supervisors being present. The idea is not to spy on the supervisors, but rather to hear directly from the employees on how things are going—with no one to filter the information.

This technique serves two important purposes. First, it keeps the GM connected to the issues and concerns of the employees, without any filters, roadblocks, or biases getting in the way. And second, it creates a mechanism for two-way communication between employees and leaders, allowing the employees to feel empowered and understood. It can be hugely motivational for the employees to know that their senior leaders care enough to spend time listening to them.

Leaders may not be able to "grant" every wish or request these employees might bring up, but they can listen and explain why or why not something is a good idea. Our recommendation is that two-ways occur on a scheduled basis—perhaps every other month or once a quarter—with randomly selected groups of employees. You may find that many good Kaizen suggestions come from these meetings. We have included some guidelines for effective two-way meetings in the Resources & Samples portion toward the end of the book—section 5.2.

EMPLOYEE EXPERIENCE

We talked about Employee Experience earlier in relation to organizational culture. It is also relevant when listening to your employee's needs and determining how to make changes that will improve the employee experience for them.

We don't need to tell you how challenging it has become to find and retain great talent. Employers must deliberately focus their attention on how to improve and maximize every interaction with their employees—from the initial recruiting to after they leave your employment. We need to work hard to make a good impression from the very beginning to the end of our relationship with an employee. We must put ourselves in the shoes of our employees and walk through the entire experience. Determine where the pain points are and fix them.

As your people are your most important resource, much leadership focus should be on this concept. Jacob Morgan has written extensively about this topic in *The Employee Experience Advantage*. He notes that there are three distinct areas of focus for EX.

1. The physical environment—for example, what does your breakroom look like? Is it a place where you would like to hang out? Where is the timeclock—is it easily accessible and in an attractive place? Do the desk chairs work and provide back support, or are tufts of fabric busting out of the seams? This might seem unimportant but trust us—if your employees have to work in an uncomfortable, run-down, or inconvenient environment, they won't be happy to come to work and they'll struggle to do their jobs well.

2. Technology—the newer generations of employees are tech-savvy, digital natives. They do not want to work for a hotel that uses paper punch timecards. Invest in appropriate technologies that enhance productivity and encourage flexibility (e.g., time-keeping systems that allow punching in with a mobile phone and lets employees view their schedules electronically). Make sure that your front desk and sales teams have up-to-date computers and high-speed Internet—otherwise, their daily tasks will become endlessly frustrating. Similarly, make sure the technology you use is well maintained and in good repair—no employee wants to deal with crashing computers or unstable wi-fi when they're trying to get work done.

3. Culture—the most important aspect of EX. Employees want a positive work environment with flexibility, clear leadership, fair compensation, and compelling careers.[8]

As you work to design your hotel's EX, make sure these three general areas are well-covered.

---

8   Jacob Morgan, *The Employee Experience Advantage*.

Other Employee Experience Ideas

Here are a number of specific EX ideas that may hold some value or significance for your staff. As you listen to your employees, be prepared for some or all of the following to come up.

FLEXIBLE SCHEDULING

One of the most powerful aspects of generational diversity is the incorporation of millennials into hotel leadership. A key strategy within this area is that of offering more flexibility, especially around work hours. In truth, this is probably something we as hotel leaders should have arrived at before, but like Einstein, we've kept doing the same old thing. It turns out that surveys indicate that every generation currently in the workplace values more flexibility in how and when they do their work. It just took the millennials to be outspoken enough to articulate the demand.

For many years, our hotel schedules have been: 7 a.m. to 3 p.m., 3 to 11 p.m. and 11 p.m. to 7 a.m. Why? Are those the best hours for all employees, or are they just the ones we're most used to? And if they aren't the best hours for our workers, what are ways we can adjust scheduling and make it more attractive for our employees? Scheduling involves putting the right people on the right jobs at the right times. For years, we have understood the last sentence to mean "right times—for the guests." Now we know that what we should take from that sentence is "right times—for the guests, employees, and hotel." Simply put—a 360-degree view of scheduling.

In the Cornell study, "Workforce Scheduling: A Guide for the Hospitality Industry," Gary Thompson shares:

As I see it, managers have three primary reasons to care about workforce scheduling, starting with employee preferences. Employees generally have distinct preferences regarding their job, including the tasks to which they are assigned, when and how long their breaks are, with whom they take breaks, with whom they are working, the time of day they work, which days off they have, and whether their days off are consecutive.[9]

Thompson goes on to explain that the goal is find "complementary" preferences within the team. Try to find a mix of employees—some who want to work evenings and weekends because they are in school. Some want to work normal daytime hours, to coincide with their children's schedules. Others are able to be very flexible and do on-call shifts. A good mix like this will help you flex your schedules, as needed. When the hotel leaders can meet most of the hour requirements for their employees, they will likely see better attendance and engagement. It may take a little more creativity when developing schedules.

Perhaps we need to consider more part-time shifts that allow employees to pursue other priorities in their lives, as well—moms who work five to six hours during the school days, students who work before or after their classes, employees with some disability challenges who cannot work a full eight-hour day, etc. Consider retirees who still want to be active but do not wish to work full-time. They can make excellent employees when assigned to roles that do not have intense physical requirements. Don't sell their technical skills short—they can and will learn to use software if needed. All of these (and many more) are examples of how adding flexibility into

---

9   Gary M. Thompson, "Workforce Scheduling: A Guide for the Hospitality Industry," *Cornell Hospitality Report 4*, no. 6 (2004): 7-55, https://scholarship.sha.cornell.edu/chrpubs/192.

your staffing and scheduling can help to fill those important gaps in your workforce. We have found that in many cases, these "non-traditional" workers stay with the hotel longer than other employees. They can truly be a gold mine of talent.

FLEXIBLE BENEFITS

Flexibility also extends into areas beyond staffing. Other areas may include: flexibility with benefits and job sharing. Is it possible for two people to share key jobs within the hotel? How about two housekeeping supervisors who share the role? How about two sales managers who job share? It may take more time to set up in the beginning but may very well be worth the effort.

We have seen various organizations get creative with their benefits dollars and create programs that meet the employees where they are. Some examples include help paying off student loans; transportation subsidies that include Lyft and Uber fares, if needed; paid parenting leave; employee wellness initiatives (e.g., an annual $200 allowance to use on health and wellness efforts—it can go to pay for a registration fee for a bike race, to offset some cost of a gym membership, or to purchase a meditation app for your phone).

Consider some of the unique benefits that you have in a hotel. Often there is a swimming pool and fitness center in a hotel—not something that is common in many other work settings. While they are there for the guests—are there any off hours or times when employees can enjoy the facilities? If you clearly define the ground rules, it can be an excellent wellness benefit at little or no extra cost.

Food is always an important element for employee retention. We are proud disciples of the "donut school of management," which teaches that if you want people to willingly attend meetings—bring donuts (or bagels, or cookies, or popcorn, or whatever)! Not only are you feeding your employees, but food also creates a more relaxed and social atmosphere. In addition, if you have food service in your hotel, offering free or discounted meals can be an outstanding way to differentiate yourself from other workplaces. This can be a critical benefit—especially for minimum-wage employees who live from paycheck to paycheck. We recall a situation in our past where this benefit was in place and management was considering eliminating it. They just about had a riot on their hands—it is a big deal to the employees.

There is no end to the creative and flexible options that are available to open minded managers. And the best part—you don't have to come up with all of the ideas yourself. Ask your employees what they value and start from there. Remember, it is what makes them happy and engaged that is important, NOT what you think is a good idea.

PAY FOR PERFORMANCE

Now, of course, we do need to talk about money. We can't tell you how many times we have heard something like, "Just pay them more and the employees will stay." We have found that to be partially true. On the one hand, adequate and competitive pay is critical for retention—especially for hourly employees who often are living on very tight budgets. It is important to know what the market rate is and then meet or exceed it over time. We have found that more-frequent, smaller increases encourage the employees to feel that they are making progress and "working their way up the ladder," which is motivating. Even 10–15 cents per hour can feel like a big change to your hourly employees. Our best advice is to be proactive—don't wait until the employee is already looking around or, worse yet, has received another job offer. Invest in some market pay data (or spend the time to compile it) and keep up to date with it. This should be a high priority for your HR team to keep on top of local market trends, as they can change rapidly.

When it comes to designing incentives, if done well, they can also help with employee satisfaction. Effective pay systems can be motivating—in some circumstances. The performance measures must be credible and be able to be influenced by the individual. Pay leads to other things that are attractive to employees (e.g., food, job security, status). Organizations must know how important pay is to the individual employee and why in order for any pay action to be effective.

A FEW GUIDELINES:

- In order to be motivating, rewards need to be at least 10–15 percent of base.

- Rewards that are tied to performance are more meaningful than when employees have no idea why they are getting compensation.

- Routine and entitlement can greatly reduce the motivational importance of an award. For example, spot bonuses every quarter become expected. Keep it special.

On the other hand, money isn't everything. As often as we've seen employees respond well to higher pay, we have also seen employees turn up their noses at higher pay when other benefits weren't present, or other factors were in play. And while we appreciate the importance of pay, we also know that it is not a true motivator beyond the short term. Lack of sufficient or fair pay causes employees to be unhappy or dissatisfied—but sufficient or fair pay alone rarely motivates the employee to perform. If pay ceases to be a problem or complaint for the employee, in the long run they will more likely find other things to complain about than become more motivated to do good work.

Let's talk a bit more about motivation.

As Frederick Herzberg discovered, higher-level needs of human beings are motivators—things like career growth, recognition of a job well done, and a sense of doing a great job. Lower-level needs of employees (safety, physical environment, or benefits), if not met, are dis-satisfiers. While the presence of motivators increases job satisfaction, a lack of negative elements does not lead to job satisfaction. In fact, a lack of negative elements, to our employees, is the bare minimum. If negative elements are present, then there's a problem that you need to fix, but if none are present, all is as it should be and they aren't obligated to do anything extra in return.[10]

For example, if the breakroom in a hotel is in disrepair and is not a place where anyone wants to hang out, it will become a source of dissatisfaction for the employees. It might even be enough to make them look for another job. Now, let's say the breakroom is remodeled and improved. It will cease to be a source of annoyance, certainly, but it will not motivate the employees to do a better job, because the condition of the breakroom is a dis-satisfier. In order to truly motivate an employee, leaders must focus more on the motivators and less on the dis-satisfiers. Here are some more examples of motivators and dis-satisfiers. Can you see how the motivators could cause employees to work harder and perform better, while the dis-satisfiers might only get them to step up until basic conditions are met?

---

10   Anneke Kuijk, "Two Factor Theory by Frederick Herzberg," toolshero, https://www.toolshero.com/psychology/theories-of-motivation/ two-factor-theory-herzberg.

Motivators (internal factors)	Dis-satisfiers (external factors)
Interesting, challenging work	Physical work environment
Responsibility	Salary & Benefits
Achievement	Policies
Recognition	Interpersonal relations
Advancement	Job security

Here's another example, one that proves that money isn't actually a motivator. In this example, the hotel manager learned it was important to match the compensation plan with intended results AND to consider the population that they were seeking to motivate with pay.

In this situation, there was a new "piece rate" pay plan for housekeepers. The goal was to increase the number of rooms that each housekeeper could clean per shift, and to pay more to those who were more efficient than others who were less so. The system was designed to eventually eliminate some team members and clean the rooms with fewer, more-productive housekeepers. It sounds like a good idea on the surface.

However, in this particular hotel, the housekeepers were predominantly Latino. Hispanic and Latino culture values relationships and loyalty—almost to the exclusion of other things. These housekeepers knew each other, and in many cases were family. The concept of working harder, maybe making more money, and possibly costing your cousin her job was not acceptable to the group. The system fell apart as they had mass exodus from the hotel—the group of housekeepers simply left together and went to another hotel. (We've seen this type of pay system fail with groups of Southeast Asian descent also for similar reasons—their strong collectivism culture did not support this type of system.)

So, don't forget about money as a key factor in your EX … but don't try to use money *as* your EX, either. Make sure you ask and listen, so you're able to give your employees the EX that works best for them, not just the one that's easiest for you to give.

CHAPTER SEVEN

WHEN THE COMFORT ZONE ISN'T

The Story

"Seriously, Josh, we have fourteen open positions and you say we can't find candidates?" Margaret and Josh were huddled in their now-weekly meeting. "We know that we need to retain people and are looking at our culture and employee experience, but we have to get them in the door first. The Housekeeping and Front Desk folks are screaming for help. These open jobs are costing us a fortune in overtime and temporary labor. Have you posted all of the jobs on our website? What about H-Careers? Did we check in with the Department of Labor?"

Josh sighed. "Of course I have. I've done all of those things. I have also put posts on Craigslist. But we're still not getting the applicant flow we need—not even half of what we need, to be honest. And that's not the worst part, either. Of the applicants we did get last week, a third of them no-showed for their interviews this week. So, we're clearly not getting the quality of applicants we want, either. I think we need to look at some new ideas."

"What about Dolores? Doesn't she have some referrals for us?" Margaret asked.

Josh barked a laugh. "Dolores says, and I quote, she 'already has a full-time job, so why don't I do mine and find her some candidates!' I think we need to get creative here; can we brainstorm a bit?"

"Well . . ." Margaret paused. "In the past, when labor was really short, I remember that focusing on our employee referral program was a big hit and was pretty successful in bringing in new candidates. I think our employees are very careful about who they refer to us."

"Okay, I like the sound of that, but that was well before my time. I'd imagine it's been quite a while since we last published the referral program. Maybe we need to update it a bit and even enhance it in this tight job market. We clearly need to talk about it with the staff more so they know it exists—Dolores certainly didn't mention it, so I wonder if she even knows about it herself."

"That makes sense. Can you look it up? What do we pay now?" Margaret asked.

Josh did a quick search through his hard drive, finding the files after a few minutes—thankfully his predecessor had been an organization nut. "Okay, here we go . . . this is at least four years old. Looks like we pay a total of $150—half up front and half after six months." Josh scratched his chin. "Does that seem low to you? I really don't think that's enough to encourage folks to even talk to people they know, let alone do any outreach."

"I agree," said Margaret. "While it's not a poke in the eye, it would not be enough to get me to do anything differently. I don't want to overreach, but I'd say at least double it for the time being.

Maybe we make it clear that the bounty is higher on an interim basis while the market is so tight and we could readjust if needed later."

"That's a good idea," agreed Josh. "I'll dig into the policy here and craft some communication around it. Maybe if I tell Dolores this will get her new workers more easily, she will help me translate it into Spanish as well. We've got quite a few Spanish-speaking employees, after all." He grabbed a pen and started scribbling notes. "Here's another thought: What do you think about making the second payment after three months rather than six months, so they see the cash sooner? I remember when I was working hourly, the sooner I could get a bonus or incentive, the more likely I was to work for it."

"I like that." said Margaret. "Let's make it happen. I'm sure between everyone under Dolores, Tiana, and Mark, there will be a bunch of friends and friends-of-friends to help us fill this gap. And don't tell me—we'll make sure everyone knows to talk about the culture and EX improvements we've been making, right?"

"You got it," said Josh. "That should give us a good starting point for heart-of-house."

Margaret looked puzzled. "Just heart of house? I know Linh needs at least one or two new sales managers, and Jose isn't quite up to filling Billy's shoes in Engineering all by himself yet. Can't we do the same kind of referral plan for those positions?"

"Well, yes and no," said Josh. "Once we get above heart of house, we need to consider the right fit a lot more than just filling positions with warm bodies. Plus, our recruiting or referral team is a lot smaller. Let's face it, it's not all that likely that a bartender or front desk employee will know an experienced chief engineer or sales manager. I mean, it *could* happen, but I've never seen it. Have you?"

"Once or twice, but that's a fair point. So what, we need to ask the managers and leadership team for higher-level referrals?"

"Right," said Josh. "And that means a higher payout. If we're going $300 for heart of house, I'd suggest at least $500 for management."

Margaret grimaced. "I don't love that, but I can see the logic. Let's make it time-bound like the $300 one, though."

"Fine with me. I'm also going to look into doing some paid advertising on LinkedIn to attract management talent, especially for Linh's sales managers. One of my mentors gave a talk about it at the last HR Directors meeting, and I think it could help a lot as well. I'm going to give it a shot."

"Don't go overboard with the ad spend, but sure," said Margaret. "And at the next staff meeting, let's present all of this and get everyone on the 'recruiting wagon.' I might even have a little fun and look Dolores in the eyes while we're having the discussion, just to make her squirm a bit."

Josh laughed so hard he almost choked on his Diet Coke, and Margaret joined in.

The Solution

Clearly, with 3.9 percent unemployment nationally (6.1 percent within the hospitality industry, as reported by the US DOL) and the federal government cracking down on the use of H2-B visa candidates, hotel employers need to approach recruiting their staff in a new way.

Everyone is a recruiter—just as everyone is a sales person for the hotel. Hotel leadership needs to be very clear about this expectation and provide the necessary tools and information.

For Heart-of-House Positions

EMPLOYEE REFERRALS

Employee referrals are the single best recruiting source for any business. Most people tend to have a network of friends who are a lot like them. If an employee has already shown that they can be successful with your hotel, then their friends are likely to be a fit, as well. However, employees need to have an incentive to put themselves out there to recruit—not only may they not consider it to be part of their job description, they also may have no idea that they *can* recruit. Either way, an incentive helps them keep recruiting in mind as they go about their lives.

First, let your employees know that you are looking for more workers, and tell them exactly what you are looking for. Not only will they need to know what roles need to be filled, but also the key characteristics that are important for your culture. Make it clear that the roles people are currently in do not need to be an exact match with the open jobs in the hotel. That is, these new workers don't *have* to come from other hotels. For example, a counter person at the local taco shop may demonstrate rock-star customer service skills—which could make them an amazing front desk agent.

Next, provide tools such as business cards with relevant contact information. Give a stack of the cards to absolutely every employee and talk about recruiting successes often, so that it inspires other employees to get in on the action.

An incentive program is another crucial piece of the strategy. "What's in it for me?" is the most common pushback to referrals. Successful employee referral or "bounty" programs can be hugely successful. The most effective programs pay the bounty in two separate installments. Part of the money is paid upon hire, with the larger component paid after some time on the job (i.e., ninety days). One common problem that we see is employers who go "too skinny" with the referral bonuses. Consider the actual cost of an unfilled job—in opportunity cost, temp fees or overtime expenses when determining the payout. Don't be too cheap with your referral payments—$25 is not going to change any one's behavior. Make it enough to encourage employees to make an effort for you.

ONLINE RESOURCES

There is some debate about whether or not Craigslist is a friend or foe when it comes to recruiting heart-of-house employees. The reality for many of us is that Craigslist is the single best online source for many entry level jobs throughout the country. It is important to continue to refresh and repost your open jobs on a regular basis. Since so many jobs are posted on Craigslist and search results are always up to date, posts older than one day are often considered stale. If you miss even one day of refreshing an ad, you may miss out on your candidate.

Now, let's talk about "keywords." Candidates may search by job title, industry, location, full- or part-time, or by specific requirements. Examples of keywords for a front desk agent position include: desk clerk, front desk, customer service, guest service, and hotel. An engineer example might include: engineer, maintenance, handyman, hotel, or apartment.

Some communities have electronic-based bulletin boards (e.g., Nextdoor.com) that can be a good source of both direct advertising and referrals.

Additional online opportunities may come from more traditional partners, such as community centers, houses of worship, and selected social agencies. They may allow you to post a job opening or a link on their website.

SOCIAL MEDIA

For these employees and their relationships, the goal is to get your good employees to help tell your story to their friends. The single best resource for this—for heart-of-house team members—is Facebook. Create a Facebook page for your hotel and keep it current. Encourage your employees to follow the hotel and to share posts with their friends. Note: these posts are not ads, they are interactive conversations. As with any conversation, the only way to get your story told is for someone to repeat it. They won't repeat it if it is not interesting and engaging. So, simply posting an ad on Facebook and then doing nothing with it is as useless as writing it on a piece of paper and then putting it in the trash. Tell your story in an interesting and engaging way. Once you have their attention, you can then tell them more about the job itself.

PRINT MEDIA

Your first reaction to print media might well be—it's old, it's tired, and it doesn't accomplish much. You may be right. But, remember our focus on doing things differently. If we look at specialized and targeted print advertising in ethnically or culturally based periodicals, for example, this can be a cost-effective and productive way to get your story told. In some cases, this will involve paying to get the ad translated into another language. Keep it visually pleasing as well—make it interesting.

JOB FAIRS

More and more employers are having success with holding job fairs—either at their facility or in a place that is convenient for the candidates. The goal is simple—get as many people in the door as possible and have a team there to do on-site interviews. Be prepared to make *contingent job offers on the spot,* so have whatever paperwork is needed. You can follow up with the I-9 checks, drug and background testing, etc., when they come in for their first training shift.

In order to attract a good crowd, hotels must be strategic in where they advertise the job fair. Community boards, social media, even billboards on mass transit can all be good ideas.

Make it a comfortable experience. Have a greeter to welcome possible candidates and to get the preliminary information. We have had good luck with serving refreshments as they fill out paperwork or wait. I've even seen events where they give transit vouchers to those who stay for an interview. Little giveaways with the hotel logo and information on it are a nice touch. Remember, it is competitive out there, so we need to make people want to work for us—not go down the street.

TRADE AND TECHNICAL SCHOOLS

Community colleges, technical schools, or trade schools can provide two different levels of resources for candidates. If the school has a dedicated hotel or hospitality program, this may be an exceptional resource for interns or management trainee candidates. All of these schools may produce entry level heart-of-house candidates through their student employment offices.

COMMUNITY RESOURCES

Some hotel employers are having good success recruiting in a really old-school manner: bulletin boards in grocery stores, community centers, and houses of worship. The traditional practice of posting a notice with tear-off contact numbers on the bottom (in the appropriate language for your target audience) is a simple but effective approach. Ask your employees where they shop, worship, and gather with their friends, and you suddenly have a good list of places to post your notice.

Most local Departments of Labor/Jobs & Training centers post available jobs. This can be a wonderful source for candidates. Be sure that your open positions are sent to the local centers on a regular basis.

Goodwill Industries are partnering with the American Hotel and Lodging Association on a national basis to train and refer entry-level hospitality candidates. This may also be true of smaller, local organizations who help to train and place individuals with various kinds of physical and learning disabilities who are able to work in some types of jobs.

TEMP TO HIRE

As the labor shortage intensifies, there is a growing need to augment your staff with temporary or contract workers. Developing a strong partnership with a temp worker provider is a critical strategy. It is important to have the ability to flex your staff up or down as needed. Make sure that the temp team knows your hotel and what you are looking for. Treat them like valued partners and they will be more likely to do their best work for you.

In most cases, there is an option to hire a temp employee on as regular staff after some period of time. Be sure that the terms of the hire are spelled out in the contract with the temp labor provider. While there is some upfront expense associated with this approach, the "try before you buy" technique may pay off with better hires.

For Management Talent

BRAND POSTINGS

Posting on your hotel's brand or property management site allows people who may already be familiar with your brand and your systems an opportunity to grow their career. This should absolutely be the first step for every professional level job posting.

REFERRALS

Once again, employee referrals are a critical source of talent at this level. As noted above, the program guidelines should be similar for these positions but with a higher prospective referral bonus.

SOCIAL MEDIA/ONLINE RESOURCES

Social media is especially powerful and important for these types of positions. The world's largest pool of professional level talent is LinkedIn. Its importance in today's competitive world of recruiting cannot be overstated. As strong as Facebook is for heart-of-house potential, LinkedIn is just as powerful for management and executive candidates.

The process for LinkedIn is much the same as Facebook. The more hotels engage, share relevant information, and enter into meaningful conversation, the more times they are exposed to a candidate pool. In addition, much like Facebook, LinkedIn also has the ability to place paid ads for open positions, using algorithms to assure that your ad directly hits your target audience.

Many hotels find value in buying a premium recruiting package that allows you to actively search for both active and passive candidates. H-Careers, Indeed, and Jobsinrichmond.com (or your city) are important resources, as well. Glassdoor has become an increasingly popular site for posting jobs.

One cautionary note here: traditionally written job postings will not be effective on these sites. Your employment postings must sell the sizzle and not the steak. In other words, focus on attracting talent rather than outlining a job description. Tell a story and make it as visual as possible. Talk about culture and EX, motivators and growth opportunities—don't just describe what a position's duties will be. The current generation of job seekers need to be quickly engaged and stimulated in order to read a post. Bullet points are better than paragraphs and action verbs create just that (to take some action). They can apply, send it to a friend, comment or share the posting—all of those actions are a good thing.

TRADITIONAL RECRUITERS

Professional recruiters may be helpful, but they do cost money. Based on our experience, the cost for engaging a traditional recruiter can be a low of 15 percent of base salary all the way up to a high of 50 percent of total first-year compensation. In most cases, this should not be your first option. If your network is strong, your online presence is good, and there is a decent active candidate pool, don't go here.

However, in an area of very low unemployment or in a market where you really need to search for passive candidates, or in the event of a confidential search, recruiters may be the appropriate choice. They may also be an option to assist with specific, hard-to-fill skills sets.

CHAPTER EIGHT

THE MISSING
PUZZLE PIECE

The Story

"Josh? Are you in there?"

"Huh?" Josh looked up blearily to see Margaret standing in front of his desk.

"I've been saying your name for two minutes straight," Margaret said, arching an eyebrow. "You were on another planet, I think."

Josh groaned and stretched his arms over his head. "Sorry. I'm a little buried right now." He pointed to the piles of job applications, resumes, and other notes that covered his desk.

"I can see that," said Margaret. "How are all the interviews coming along? Are you finding the people that we need? Remember, we're looking for culture fit as well as skills!" She started to laugh but trailed off when Josh didn't join her. Margaret sat down. "Okay, what's the matter? You really aren't acting like yourself. Talk to me."

Josh ran his fingers through his hair. "Well, the truth is that my being buried here isn't a joke. It's what, three thirty now? I've been digging through all this since eleven and I'm getting nowhere. I love that our referral program is working so well, but it feels like we've just exchanged that problem for an even bigger one—one that lands squarely on my desk. We've been doing so much interviewing that I can barely keep track of all the candidates, let alone evaluate them as individuals. Did you know I interviewed five engineers yesterday?" He made a vague gesture to one of the resume piles. "I couldn't tell you which one was which today. This process is a *lot* more complicated than my last hotel's was—then again, they were half the size of Capitol House and never had this many positions open all at once."

Margaret held up a hand before her clearly exhausted HR director could start to ramble. "Okay, hold up for a second. First of all, I want you to know that I'm really happy with how we've gone from too many open positions to too many interviews. That's a much better problem to have, even if it feels like all *your* problem." Josh nodded a weary thanks. "But I think it's my turn to challenge you on something here. You mentioned a process, but I see no evidence of any kind of process when I look at your desk right now. It mostly just looks like chaos. I think you need to step back and build some consistent tools that you can use across all candidates to keep track of things and to compare apples to apples."

Josh looked at his desk, then at Margaret, then back, his face slowly turning red. "Yeah, about that. You're right. I know better than this. Even at my last hotel there were tools for this—interview guides, applicant scoring grids, that kind of thing. I just didn't think about any of that. Wow. I totally messed this up, didn't I?"

Margaret leaned forward to meet Josh's gaze "I'm not trying to make you feel badly. You have done a great job of selecting new employees before now, and I'm sure you'll keep doing it. I just think that the current volume of open jobs and candidates requires a new level of organization and defined processes. You know me, I am a big fan of defined processes!"

"You're right. We need to get our arms around this and make it much more systematic. Maybe that will help keep things on track and keep us from making hiring mistakes. I think there have been a couple of instances lately where Tiana has 'fallen in love' with some front desk candidates that I don't think are a good fit for us. But I really was not able to articulate good reasons *not* to hire them. And she was desperate for bodies so she went ahead."

"You need to step back, map out the workflow and build some systems and tools to make this process more effective," cautioned Margaret. "I want you to work from home one day this week and spend it creating new workflows and some tools to help you out. Because it's not just you that needs these things—you mentioned Tiana wasn't on the same page with you, and if she isn't, then I imagine Linh and Jose and the rest could use some guidance, too. When you bring these tools back, I'll give you the next staff meeting to present them to everyone. Okay?"

Josh squinted at Margaret for a moment. "Who are you and what have you done with my boss?"

Margaret laughed. "Yeah, I know. Actually I'm pretty proud of myself for coming up with that! Even this old leopard can change its spots sometimes, right?"

Josh shook his head. "You could say that, sure. And I definitely feel better now that I have a path to make some order out of this chaos—especially with your support. Thanks a lot, seriously."

"You're welcome. Now go home, get some sleep, and start that path in the morning."

The Solution

Remember the first principle of Lean: everything is a process, and every process can be improved. Effective hiring is no different—it is a process and it can be improved with a systematic, repeatable approach. Advance preparation is one key to success—just like in most other aspects of life. The goal is to create a solid, repeatable process that will help to identify the "right fit" candidates.

Balanced Hiring Process

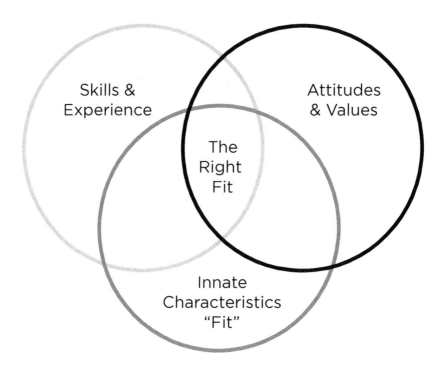

Finding the right candidate can sometimes feel like looking through a mound of puzzle pieces looking for the right one. While the screening and interviewing of candidates is often considered an "art," this process should actually be considered much more of a "science." We will approach this process from a very systematic and strategic approach to the hiring process.

Many folks believe they have the secret sauce to hiring because they "know the right fit when they see it." More often than not, this creates the process of "falling in love with a candidate" and not allowing yourself to truly see the candidate's strengths and weaknesses—which oftentimes causes us to hire a candidate that we *like* rather than the candidate with the best chance of success. In this chapter, we carefully review the seven steps of the screening and interviewing process as well as identify tools and resources that will make the process smoother for hiring managers. Note that while the need is different for management positions versus heart-of-house positions, the basic interviewing process is the same.

Step One—Define the Position

The basis for any hiring process is a thoughtful and well-defined job description. This is a document that describes the general tasks and other related duties or responsibilities of a position. It may specify who the position reports to, the qualifications or skills needed by the person in the job, and a salary range. Job descriptions are usually narrative, but some may comprise a simple list of competencies.

Job descriptions for management positions may vary significantly from heart-of-house positions. Heart-of-house positions might list the basic skills required and align those with the duties required and expected performance levels. Management positions must be broader and may have duties across multiple areas or "buckets." Below are examples that are generic to multiple management level positions and may be incorporated into the process for various different departments.

Examples of buckets may include:

- Culture

  - Foster spirit of teamwork

  - Consciously create a workplace culture that is consistent with the overall organization

  - Maintain transparent communication

- Scheduling and Staffing

  - Plan staffing levels

  - Maintain employee work schedules including:

    - ✓ Assignments

    - ✓ Job rotation

    - ✓ Training

    - ✓ Vacations

    - ✓ PTO (Paid Time Off)

    - ✓ Telecommuting

    - ✓ Overtime Scheduling

- Talent Management

  - Work with Human Resources to recruit, interview, select, and hire the appropriate number of employees

  - Provide oversight and direction to employees in accordance with policies and procedures

  - Delegate responsibility and expect accountability and regular feedback

- Performance Feedback and Team Member Development

- Coach, mentor, and develop staff, including overseeing new employee onboarding and providing career development planning and opportunities

- Empower employees to take responsibility for their jobs and goals

- Lead employees using a performance management and development process that provides overall context and framework

  ✓ Goal Setting

  ✓ Feedback

  ✓ Performance

It is not uncommon for the list of "requirements" for the job to be really long—something like a Christmas gift list. Remember that perfect candidates seldom exist. Search firms call that the "unicorn syndrome"—searching for something that is rare, special, and likely make believe. At this point, you might want to ask, "Should I be accepting 'non-perfect' candidates?" The reality-based answer is YES. In truth, there are no "perfect" candidates. If we utilize a systematic approach to reading applications and resumes with consistency, we then proceed with those candidates who score most closely to perfect.

When viewed with this lens, we see that there may be candidates who aren't perfect but who will still help us move forward. As we discussed in an earlier chapter, the phrase "don't let great get in the way of good" applies here. Do not pass on a good candidate just hoping to find the "unicorn."

"PERFORMANCE" LEVEL CANDIDATES VERSUS "POTENTIAL" LEVEL CANDIDATES

So, it's tradeoff time when determining the really essential criteria for selection. This may be a good time to consider the long-term potential of an employee rather than simply looking at their previous work experience in a similar or related role. Rather, think about an individual in that job who has been successful. What key characteristics did that person have? It is likely something more like a positive attitude, a willingness to do whatever it takes, flexibility, great problem-solving skills, a calm demeanor, a solid work ethic, etc. Notice that none of these criteria are exclusively the result of previous job experience. It may be helpful for you to identify a short list of attributes (which become your selection criteria) like those we listed that are essential for success in the job. High-potential applicants who have many of these attributes may also have an increased likelihood of being promotable into more responsible roles in the future.

Step Two—Write Ads That Attract

As we discussed in the previous chapter—what this means today is very different from what this has meant in the past.

Specific strategies for assuring touchpoints into this demographic include:

- Get your team to tell their story to their friends and networks

- Embrace social media

- Collaborate more—direct less

- Offer more flexibility

- Communicate differently and more quickly

Specific attention needs to be paid to writing ads or social media posts that attract the talent we need. While ads that are basic "job descriptions" have historically worked, today we find that they often do more harm than good. What is wanted in today's job market are ads that:

- Have content relative to them

- Sell first, explain later

- Tell a story

- The NANOSECOND format

- Get them to ACT, even if they don't apply

Simplified, we must remember that to attract the talent we want, we have to meet them where they are. Speak to them in the ad, don't write a job description. The NANOSECOND format reminds us that they should be able to scan the ad quickly and it must catch their attention and get them to act, even if they don't apply. What is meant by that is that, even if this position is not right for the person reading it at the time, it may very well be perfect for one of their friends or other folks in their social network. So, even if they don't apply, but they forward, tell someone, or otherwise share it, then the goal has still been accomplished.

See more information on ads that attract in the back of the book.

Step Three—Create Evaluation Tools

The purpose of a standardized evaluation tool is to ensure that you compare apples to apples when evaluating how well a candidate fits with your selection criteria. It helps to use a consistent scoring metric. This will also help prevent less sophisticated managers from "falling in love" with a candidate—someone with whom they connected with but who may not have the requisite skills and abilities to do the job.

Think back to those essential characteristics and pick the top five or six (not more). **Prioritize and assign weights to the competencies and experiences**. This underscores the point that not all requirements are created equal—some are more critical than others. In order to assign weightings to the competencies you have identified, ask yourself the following questions:

- What competencies *must* people have in order to be effective on the job? (These will be the position's primary requirements.)

- What competencies would be helpful, but can be developed on the job? (These will be the secondary requirements for the job.)

- What competencies might be good additions or bonuses to the job, but aren't strictly necessary to performing it? (These will not be requirements for the job, but may be used to help decide between applicants with similar grades.)

The most valuable competencies will receive the heaviest weight in your scale, and the applicants who meet those criteria the closest will get the highest grade. Now, you have identified your *selection criteria* for hiring.

Once you have identified this hiring criteria and how you will "grade" an applicant, it is time to look at resumes—using this information as the lens.

Step Four—Grade Applicants and Resumes

Driven by the first step in the cycle, clearly defining the position is the key. When we've taken the time to do our homework on the front end, grading by metrics becomes simple:

- An **A** candidate meets ALL the primary requirements and most of the secondary requirements of the job; they may also meet several bonus criteria.

- A **B** candidate meets most of the primary requirements and some of the secondary requirements of the position; they may meet one or two bonus criteria, as well.

- A **C** candidate meets some of the primary requirements and few of the secondary requirements of the position; they probably won't meet any bonus criteria.

- An **F** candidate does not meet either the primary or secondary requirements of the position and should be passed on, OR be considered for another position that might more appropriately match their background and skill set

Also, bear in mind that matching an applicant's resume to your list of primary, secondary, and bonus requirements may not be intuitive. As you read over resumes, look for evidence of those criteria in some of the following areas:

- Ability to sell self—tell a story

  - Is there a logical flow?

  - Can you easily understand their career path?

- Evidence of qualifications/experience

- Are specific qualifications (i.e., PMS, staffing, time management, or sales systems) easily identifiable?

- Employment history—unexplained gaps

  - Missing dates (i.e., return to school, job transitions, etc.) should be easily understood.

- Sloppiness/organization

  - Document should be free from typos, and grammatical and punctuation errors.

  - Telephone numbers and email addresses should be easily located.

- Educational background

  - Resume should clearly indicate schools/universities attended and degrees received.

Once the resumes or applications have been reviewed and graded, candidates should immediately be scheduled for interviews. If enough A candidates are not available, then move on to B candidates. Ideally, you'll be able to fill the position before you need to go to C candidates, but keep their resumes on file, just in case.

Step Five—Interview Strategically

As mentioned earlier in this chapter, successful hiring comes from having more science than art to the selection and hiring process. The key to strategic interviewing is simple: consistency. Consistency in the questions asked, consistency in follow-through and clarifying questions, consistency in note-taking and follow-up, and consistency in grading the interview.

When you ask all the candidates for the job relatively similar questions, you can easily and effectively compare and contrast their responses. In order to do that, you must again plan ahead and create patterned interviews or interview guides. The beauty of these is that once they have been created for a position, they can be used over and over again. This practice will streamline the process of preparing for interviews for the foreseeable future of your hotel.

QUESTIONS TO ASK

Behavioral-based interviewing is founded on the premise that "the best predictor of future behavior is past behavior under similar circumstances." In contrast to theoretical questions, competency-focused questions are more effective in predicting how a candidate will perform on the job.

Theoretical questions are hypothetical in nature (what an applicant says he/she *might* do). While the answer may sound great, it is not actually representative of what the candidate would actually do in the real situation. An example of a theoretical question would be: How would you handle a disgruntled customer?

Behavioral focused questions seek *demonstrated* examples of behavior from past experience (that is, what a candidate *has done* rather than what they might do). The interviewee's answers typically contain references to specific names, dates, places, the outcome and their role in achieving that outcome.

Behavioral based questions are based on past experiences and often are phrased along these lines:

"Tell me about . . ."

"Give me a specific example of a time when you . . ."

"Describe for me . . ."

"Describe your experience with . . ."

"What did you do . . ."

"What would you do differently . . ."

"Think of an occasion when you . . ."

Follow-up questions might be:

"What was the result?"

"Tell me more about the role **you** *played."*

When planning your interview questions, also remember not to ask any questions that you can find the answers to on the applicant's resume. It is a waste of both the candidate's time and yours and proclaims loudly that you did not actually read the resume in the first place.

Sample questions that will support this process for management candidates might include:

- Can you describe a time when you proactively identified and addressed an issue at your hotel?

- How do you set long-term goals for your team? How often do you check and review these goals?

- Can you describe a time when you failed to achieve your goals and had to follow a different approach? What happened?

- What are the key factors you take into consideration when building an action plan?

Sample questions that will support the process for heart-of-house candidates might include:

- What does good guest service mean to you?

- Can you describe a time when you had to deal with an unhappy guest? How did you handle the situation?

- Can you describe a time you had to disappoint a guest? What was the situation and how did you handle it?

- Let's say your to-do list has five tasks and you only have time for three. How would you prioritize them?

- A guest asks you for local restaurant and entertainment suggestions. Where would you recommend if they were a single business traveler, young couple, or family with children?

QUESTIONS YOU SHOULD NOT ASK—ERRORS TO AVOID

Leading Questions

Avoid using leading questions, which suggest to the applicant the preferred or expected response.

"I'll bet you had to be patient and listen carefully to the customer, didn't you?"

"You must have put in a lot of extra hours to get all that work done on time?"

Close-ended Questions

Close-ended questions elicit a simple "yes" or "no" answer. They offer no behavioral data.

"Did you arrive on time?"

"Did you analyze all of the options before making the decision?"

Once you have developed your interview guide and evaluation tool, we suggest that you create spaces for writing notes right on the guide and print out enough copies to use for each interview. Keep your notes and thoughts well organized right on the guide. It will make comparing and contrasting the various candidates a much easier task.

Step Six—Testing and Predictive Indexes

One of the best, but most overlooked, pieces of the cycle is the testing and assessment component. Successful hotels and organizations take the time to understand who their most successful team players are, both at the management level as well as in heart of house; and then recruit more candidates who model those successes. Hospitality employers need to focus not only on filtering out a candidate who won't perform, but also on hiring candidates who are the best fit for the organization and job so they are likely to stay for a longer period. This makes having pre-employment tests for promising applicants hugely important.

Here's what you need to do to set up these tests:

1. Clearly identify your most successful team members for each area or position

2. Identify a personality test or assessment tool that will measure the candidates against these successful team members. There are many good quality, valid instruments in the market. Standardized testing products that are widely available include:

    ✓ Personality Testing

    ✓ Integrity Testing

    ✓ General Mental Ability Testing.

3. Once you complete the initial screening and interview process and narrow the field to the best potential new hires, ask each candidate to take the test. (Only testing the final applicants allows for cost savings during the hiring process.)

4. Evaluate the test results for each applicant, and move on to the final step based on those results. Recall that the testing is only one indicator of success—there are not pass or fail results, just more data so that you can make a more-informed selection decision.

5. Finally, the results of these kinds of assessments can be helpful in determining how to manage the new employee once they have been hired. Be sure that your hiring manager gets to see the results and talk with them about how it might impact the on-boarding of the new employee.

Step Seven—Hire Right

Easy to say, not always easy to accomplish! Finding "that missing puzzle piece" requires as much time and dedication as actually putting a many thousand-piece jigsaw puzzle together. If you have taken the time to follow each step of the cycle, then you should find the right puzzle piece every time. We have found that the quality of the hire is usually directly linked to the time we put into the hiring process.

Resist the urge to just hire warm bodies to fill your vacancies—the problems that cause in the long run make it a short-term fix at best.

Remember, our goal is to attract and retain the BEST people.

CHAPTER NINE

SINK OR SWIM?

The Story

Margaret plopped down into the chair across from Josh's desk and grinned widely at him. "Ask me how I am today!"

Josh was confused. "Say what?"

"Ask me how I am today! Come on, just ask me!"

"Okay: How are you today, Margaret?"

Margaret all but bounced in her chair. "I'm doing *great!* Our turnover is down substantially and our GSS scores are starting to creep back up! I am really seeing some signs of life here!"

Josh grinned back at his boss. "Didn't think we'd get there when we first started all this a few months ago, did you?"

"No, I sure didn't, but I'm glad you helped me open my mind to it all," said Margaret. "Telling people what we expected has helped us create a more consistent environment. Heck, I even see employees smiling now when they work—and not just in front of guests, either!"

"Yes, things are going much better," Josh agreed. "I'm also pretty pumped about the Kaizen teams that we have sponsored. The employees have identified some really excellent suggestions on how to make things more efficient. That new process for standardizing how the housekeeping carts are stocked is nothing short of brilliant."

Margaret nodded. "As much as I hate to admit it, the old 'do it because I said so' style of management doesn't seem to go over very well with our newer employees. I have to give you credit—you were right about asking for more input from them and letting our team be part of the solution to some of our problems." She paused for a moment, and cracked a smile. "But it's not always as fun as just telling folks what to do was!" They both laughed briefly.

"Okay," said Margaret. "I'm sure it's not all sunshine and roses around here. What fire do we need to put out this week?"

Josh's smile turned rueful. "Well, we have another problem within Housekeeping. The recruiting bonus was super helpful and I was really excited about the four new housekeepers that we hired. I was hoping that we could back off on using the temp workers soon. But two of the four have resigned already."

"That does seem like a setback. What do you think is going on?"

"It could be a couple of different things," Josh replied. "The two who just left complained about a lack of training—Dolores gave them a hard time about not cleaning rooms the right way, but never actually taught them what that way was. One also felt that Dolores was playing favorites. I know that we have heard that second one before and I have talked to Dolores about fairness and equity several times. I'm not sure if she really is favoring the Latino employees or if her ability to speak to them in Spanish is misinterpreted by the others. So I'm thinking it's probably some of both issues—and they may be exacerbating each other."

Margaret frowned. "Fair enough. Well, let's dig into each of these complaints separately. What kind of training or orientation do we provide to new housekeepers now?"

Josh found himself trying not to feel defensive. "Well, to be honest, creating a hotel-wide on-boarding program has been on my radar for some time and I just have not had the time to get to it. I'm spending so much time trying to find and hire people."

Margaret couldn't help but grin again. "So, are you saying that you think you need to improve this process all by yourself? Isn't that the problem that we are trying to cure with our team—to realize that we are all accountable for our culture and that we will involve the employees to help solve problems? Is this a case of 'preaching to the choir?'"

"Yeah, I think you got me on this one," Josh admitted. "Our on-boarding is a problem and we can't wait any longer to address it. I don't think it has changed in years and I know better. We are hiring more folks with less experience and higher expectations around training and development. We need to do a much better job of equipping them to succeed. A lot of them simply don't understand what we expect of them. It often tends to be a sort of sink-or-swim approach with new people around here. I can't believe I let this slide as long as I have."

"Don't beat yourself up—at least not too much. Sounds like a job for a new Kaizen team, for sure. Let me ask a different question. Why do you suppose it is harder to do this effective on-boarding in housekeeping than it is with bartenders? Or front desk agents? I don't recall Mark or Tiana getting these kinds of complaints."

Josh thought for a moment. "Maybe it is because we buddy them up with another bartender or desk agent for quite a few shifts before letting them go solo. I wonder if we could do something like that with housekeeping, too. It's definitely worth thinking about. Let's put it to the team. And I have a pile of good information about on-boarding ideas that I have picked up from some of my HR association meetings. Looks like it's time to dig out those files."

"I think you should also take a look at everything that is on your plate," Margaret said. "Maybe there are some things that can be delegated to Kimbr or other folks on the team."

Josh nodded. "Yeah, I'm not great at this delegation stuff. It usually seems faster to just do it myself." Margaret opened her mouth but Josh continued, "And yes, I know that I am continuing to create the problem when I don't help other people learn how to do some of these tasks. I'm giving them the answer instead of teaching them to fend for themselves. I'll ask Kimbr who I could offload some research to."

"Good," said Margaret. "Now, what about the favoritism issue?"

"We have heard these complaints about favoritism in the past, but I don't think Dolores does it intentionally. I think she is just more comfortable with our Hispanic employees because she's Hispanic herself. I can try to talk with her again, but really I think this may be a future training opportunity. She needs to understand both her unconscious biases and that one size does not fit all when managing people. Each person has unique needs and she needs to flex to deal with them—not the other way around. She has to get to know each of them as an individual and to understand what issues, concerns, strengths, and weaknesses each person has.

"And that's not just true of Dolores, we're all in that boat. We have to realize that people bring their whole selves to work—their problems don't just stay outside the hotel! Until we realize that, people will not feel that we are treating them with respect."

"Wow," said Margaret. "I had no idea you were so passionate about this, Josh. And you know what—it makes me think about that day a few weeks back when I made Dolores discipline that nice young house-person who looked like she had slept in her uniform. I realize now that I didn't ask any questions or try to understand what was going on with that young woman. I just reacted—and not very nicely at that. That doesn't feel good at all—I was definitely part of the problem rather than the solution there."

Josh nodded. "What would you do differently now?"

"Well, for starters I'd ask if that person were still working here, and if she were, I'd try to find out more of her story. The next time you talk to Dolores, could you follow up on the situation? If there's something I can do to make it right, I will."

"Sure, I can do that."

The Next Day

"This is Margaret," said the Capitol House GM as she picked up her office phone.

"It's Josh. I happened to talk with Dolores this afternoon, and you really need to hear this."

Margaret put down her coffee cup. "What is it?"

"It turns out that Elyse, the house-person you asked me to follow up on, not only *looked* like she slept in her uniform the other week but that she *had in fact* slept in it. She is homeless and is living in her car. When Dolores and I sat down to talk with her, she just started sobbing and asking us not to fire her!"

Margaret's heart sank. "Oh no, that poor girl. What happened to her?"

"Once we got her to calm down and talk to us, we learned that her boyfriend kicked her out of the apartment when they broke up.

She is trying to save up some cash for a deposit on a new place but needs a few checks in order to do that. I felt so helpless. I wish she had said something sooner."

"Wow, now I really feel like crap," Margaret said. "That makes any issues I have with my own adult daughter sure feel like first-world problems right now. What did you do?"

"I hooked her up with our Employee Assistance Program and they helped her connect with a resource for emergency housing. Dolores told her to take the rest of the day off—paid, of course—to meet with them and get a temporary place to live." Josh paused, and then went on with a smile, "And, you will never guess this one— Dolores offered to take her uniform home tonight and to wash and iron it for Elyse. I just about started to cry myself. That is going to send a big message to our housekeeping team—especially the non-Spanish speaking ones, since Elyse isn't Hispanic."

"Wow!" said Margaret. "I can't believe that. It sounds like Dolores is really getting the message now."

"Well, that and I think Dolores was pretty embarrassed that she had no idea of the issues Elyse was dealing with. I have to admit, after we were done talking with her, I did sneak in a comment about the importance of one-on-one meetings with all of her team members. I think she is starting to see the light on that habit."

"Thank you for dealing with this, Josh" Margaret said. "It sounds like you handled it really well. I hope things turn around for Elyse. This may be a dumb question, but do you think that this kind of issue is a problem with other employees? Do they actually have the basic life skills—things that you and I might take for granted—that keep them from being really successful at work? Maybe our new employee training needs to include more than just how to do their jobs. Maybe, we need to think about how to provide our employees with the resources that they need to succeed in life first, and then they will be better able to succeed in their jobs!"

"That is an amazing idea," Josh stated. "I'm not going to lie, I never thought I would hear those words coming from your mouth! Congrats for trying to put yourself in their shoes. Let's bring up this idea—not using names, of course—at our next management team meeting."

The Solution

The labor market is tight and you've worked hard to find and hire the right person. That's great, but your job is not done! If you've ever started a new job, only to find the company totally unprepared for your arrival, you know how important onboarding is to the employee-employer relationship!

However, in some organizations, onboarding is often confused with orientation. *Orientation* is getting the employee ready to start working. *Onboarding* is ensuring that they start successfully enough that they don't end up stopping (i.e., quitting or getting fired) after a few short days, weeks, or months. While orientation is short and sweet—paperwork and other routine tasks must be completed up front—onboarding is a comprehensive process, involving management and other employees as well as the new hire, that can last up to three months.

Doing onboarding right isn't just about making someone feel welcome or showing them the ropes. Those things are important, but they're just the beginning. Onboarding is about helping that new hire have the best chance to be successful—which is in both your best interest and theirs. "Sink or swim" is never a great approach to onboarding new employees—no longer can we simply give new hires a company manual and assume they're fully equipped for success.

This approach is even more important in this full employment market. We are all having to hire employees more for potential rather than for significant relevant experience. We cannot assume that new employees understand our expectations, or that they have the necessary skills to be successful. Just like with interviewing, a little up-front planning can turn onboarding into a highly successful experience.

As we've mentioned a few times now, clear expectations are critical. Hotel leaders cannot assume that employees understand what success looks like. Unless we tell them, each will have their own definition of what a professional hotel employee is. We must be very clear in defining our culture and code of conduct, but also in setting clear standards for success in each role within the hotel. Well-written job descriptions are an important start, but they must then be coupled with clear success factors for each role. What does success look like in each job, and how do the employees get there? (For example, how many minutes should each housekeeper spend cleaning a regular room?) Tell supervisors about your expectations on how often they have one-on-one meetings with their staff, and when they need to do formal performance evaluations. Be sure that every new employee has a copy of the job description (which is ideally given to them during the interviewing process).

An important (and sad) reality is that many hotel employees (especially heart-of-house workers) are coming from tough situations. Some have limited resources or difficult living conditions. Others may lack basic life skills that job descriptions may take for granted. These issues make performing successfully at a job a struggle and may prevent it entirely. Creative employers are now incorporating basic life skills training into their onboarding processes. Everything from how to manage a bank account to how to properly wash and dry a uniform may be helpful and new information to the employees. We need to meet the employees where they are—not where we wish them to be.

In addition to internal resources, there are often good resources in the community—various nonprofits, your EAP provider, healthcare providers, etc., who can come in and talk with the employees about these kinds of life skills. In the past, we have had health insurance contracts that included financial wellness education as well as physical wellness education for our employees at no additional charge. Other, similar opportunities may be available for your hotel.

Life skills training is not an area in which you need to be the expert—you just need to find those experts and provide access to them. Also, be sensitive when offering this type of training—don't mandate it or tell people that they should attend. Telling everyone they need to learn how to balance a checkbook will offend those who already know, but make that training available and safe to attend with no pressure either way, and many will do so.

This type of training almost always needs to be accompanied by basic job skills training. If we want the housekeepers to know how to fold clean corners on the sheets—we need to teach them how. Develop or invest in a comprehensive skills training program for job categories with multiple employees and higher turnover (housekeeping, engineering, front desk, etc.). Remember to keep it as visual as possible with short learning modules and hands-on practice. We have found it beneficial to have current staff become subject matter experts on various topics and then oversee some of the training of new hires themselves. It makes them feel good to teach the others how to perform the task—and ensures that no one's performance slips over time. This can be short training sessions that take place for five to ten minutes once a week during the daily huddles. We have included a sample of a basic-skills training curriculum at the end of this chapter.

Supervisors need to understand that it is their job to ensure that a robust and standardized onboarding happens for every employee. While the supervisor may delegate some of the training tasks to others, he or she is accountable to make sure it happens. The good news is that busy supervisors don't need to reinvent the wheel each and every time, and leadership has a tool to hold the supervisors accountable. Onboarding checklists can be very valuable to ensure consistent experiences for all new employees. See a sample at the end of the book.

Utilizing a buddy system—matching experienced employees up with new employees for a period of sixty to ninety days—can be a particularly strong win-win solution. The more-senior employee feels valued and takes some accountability to ensure that the new person gets up to speed quickly. The new employee has a built-in resource to use as needed. Note that the buddy is not the official trainer or direct supervisor. A new housekeeping hire, for example, would be "buddied up" with Housekeeper 1 or 2 with at least six months experience at the hotel, not the Housekeeping Manager. The buddy is someone to share all of the unspoken norms and cultural nuances with the new person to shorten the learning cycle. It is also a way to help the new employee feel welcomed and that they have a "friend" at work.

Tell both the new employee and the buddy what is expected. The buddy should check in with their new hire daily at first, then weekly, and finally, monthly as needed. The buddy goes to lunch with the new employee in the first week or two (with the hotel picking up the tab) and shows them the ropes regarding daily tasks like clocking in and out. The buddy becomes the first call for help—before the new employee has to get the supervisor involved. It often feels "safer" to ask a buddy rather than admit to your supervisor that you don't know something.

Choosing buddies to help new employees can be recognition for a job well done and, if done properly, can be something of a status symbol for the employee. Make a big deal of it and thank the buddies for their assistance. Sometimes a little acknowledgement (like a small gift card) can help keep the buddies engaged.

The On-Boarding Plan

The following are some thoughts on how to create an on-boarding plan.

BEFORE THE NEW HIRE STARTS WORK

- **Create a new hire checklist.** It is easy to "get too busy" to remember everything that you should provide for a new employee. By taking the time in advance to create a checklist, you can ensure that critical things are covered. Plus, this checklist can be used over and over again— and be improved over time. It can work well to have a checklist that both the employee and the supervisor need to complete and ultimately sign off on when complete. As you create the plan, don't forget to assign accountability for each action item.

- **Create an agenda for your new employee's first week.** It's much easier to plan this in advance than it is to come up with it while the new team member is standing there in front of you. If you aren't sure what to include on this agenda, reach out to the new hire's soon-to-be supervisor or other key coworkers to determine what is important. If you assign mentors or work buddies, this is a great time do that as well.

- **Create a comfortable work space for your new staff member.** Nothing kills a new employee's confidence in the company faster than being assigned to a dirty, unorganized work space. Setting up the workstation in advance gives new hires their own "turf," helping them feel more relaxed and confident. This can be as basic as having a clean locker for their things, a uniform, and a name tag ready to go.

- **Provide new employees with a welcome gift.** To help the new hire immediately feel like part of the team, gather up any appropriate branded materials such as a custom t-shirt, a hat, a coffee mug, pens, or a pad of paper. Not only will this build brand loyalty right away, it also helps a new employee feel welcomed.

- **Send out helpful information in advance.** Help soothe a new employee's first-day jitters by clearly communicating any information that's needed for the first day. Include details on dress code, parking rules, directions to the employee entrance, and who to ask for when upon arrival to minimize new hire stress. This can easily be done via text or email before the start date.

DURING THE FIRST WEEK

- **Help new hires get the lay of the land.** On the new hire's first day, conduct a tour of the hotel. Be sure to include simple, but essential, information such as where their locker is located and where the restrooms and break room are. Introduce the new employee to other staff members along the way and encourage questions as you go. If the manager/supervisor is not available on the first day, assign someone else to be accountable for this critical task.

- **Block off time for orientation**. If you're in desperate need of help, it can be tempting to throw your new employee into projects as quickly as possible. But doing so can be disorienting and nerve wracking—two feelings you definitely want to avoid for your new hire if possible. Use the new hire's first day as more of an orientation day than a work day. Try to have some current team members take breaks or have lunch with the new employee, and set aside time for filling out paperwork, introductory meetings, and casual conversation.

- **Plan a manager's meeting**. Sometime during the first week, set aside time for the new hire to meet with their immediate manager/supervisor. Use this meeting to give the manager time to get to know the new team member, share their management style, and explain future expectations. It can also be helpful to use this time to let the new employee know what the ramp-up process will be like in the first week or two on the job.

- **Cover important work processes**. As the new hire's first week progresses, have the new employee and supervisor meet a few more times as needed to discuss important work processes. For example, new staff members need to know all of the relevant safety protocols, communication expectations, and internal decision-making processes. They also need demos on how to use various technology, tools, and equipment that they'll be using on a daily basis. This is also a great time to review and set performance expectations.

- **Assign a peer buddy.** Peer buddies can be an important part of the on-boarding process. Remember, these are not trainers, they are the people who are assigned to be the "first call for help" and to whom the new employee can go for simple questions. The peer buddy should be encouraged to stop by and check in periodically and help introduce the new employee to others.

THE FIRST THIRTY TO SIXTY DAYS

- **Invest in training.** Though the productivity losses can be frustrating, a new hire's first thirty to sixty days on the job should be looked at as an initial training period. Train your new employee on everything he or she needs to know about the role.

- **Allow for job shadowing.** One of the best ways to train your new hires is to have them shadow other workers—potentially their peer buddies. But don't just focus on those in the employee's department. Cross-training your workers by having them shadow employees in other areas will give them a much better understanding of how your hotel works.

- **Build opportunities for feedback into the employee's first couple of months on the job.** Make sure new hires know that they're free to share and encourage new ideas. They may not be comfortable doing so the first day, but over time, their feedback and insights should be encouraged.

- **Conduct your first review.** Finally, after ninety days on the job, the manager should give the new hire their first evaluation. At this point, the new employee should be fully integrated into the hotel and operating at a full workload. Identifying weaknesses at this stage will allow you to either nip potential problems in the bud or terminate the new hire's employment before too many resources have been invested in an employee that won't ultimately work out.

Recall that your goal is to find and develop employees who are a good fit with your culture. When you find the right folks, they are worth gold to you. We encourage you not to make the mistake of assuming that once you get them hired, it's all an easy flow from there. In reality, on-boarding is a key but a too-often-overlooked practice. As you fine-tune your employee experience, this step is essential. After all, you only get one opportunity to make a first impression—make it a good one.

CHAPTER TEN

GROWING YOUR GANG!

The Story

Josh and Margaret were just finishing up his six-month performance review (a relatively new process that they have implemented to give more timely feedback to employees). "Things have definitely turned around and I want to again express my appreciation for your major role in that," Margaret summarized. "Is there anything else you want to discuss?"

"Well, I am really loving my job now and I like our partnership. Things feel really good—I especially get a kick out of watching your face as you struggle to keep open minded to some of the employee suggestions!" he laughed.

As if on cue, Margaret made a face.

"But seriously, I do want to talk to you about the workload around here now that things have picked up. I realize that it's a 'be careful what you wish for' issue—we wanted more business and we got it! More business means more work for everyone and the work hours around here have gotten to be killer. What used to be regular happy hours with my friends are just about non-existent these days. And my bike has a layer of dust on it. I know that it's not just me— the other leadership team members are all working the same long hours. I think we are all getting a little burned out.

"I know we talked about delegating more, and Kimbr's admins have been helping with that, but I think we need to go further. Let's look at our staffing at the leadership level. I know that there used to be an assistant general manager in the hotel and that when the last one left, the decision was made that we couldn't afford to replace it. The job tasks got kind of broken up among the team. I realize that Haversham has not completely stopped micromanaging us, but would you consider talking to him about adding the job back in now?"

"I have been thinking about the same thing," said Margaret. "It will cost money, but having someone in that role, and letting the other leadership folks really focus on their core jobs might be the just the ticket to take the hotel to the next level. Can you dig up the old job description and spend some time thinking about how you suggest that we re-distribute the responsibilities if we add it back in?"

"I'll do that and also spend some time defining what type of person it should be." Josh hesitated, then added one more thought, "And Margaret, if we do add in an AGM role, will you be able to let go of some things and delegate them to the new person? You do kind of like to do things yourself, and working with an AGM isn't the same as directing an admin."

Margaret held up her hand to stop Josh before he got really wound up. "I know what you're saying. I do like to have things done my way and am not always great about letting go. I promise to try my best."

Two weeks later, Margaret was feeling pretty pumped after her conversation with Mr. Haversham. With the RevPAR (Revenue per Available Room) up and the solid calendar of event bookings coming up, he agreed that she could look at adding back the AGM role. She picked up her phone and dialed Josh's extension.

"Josh, I just got off the phone with Mr. Haversham. He said that with RevPAR being up and our event calendar booked out for the next quarter now, he's a lot more comfortable with the AGM idea. I've made a few edits to the description you put together, but not many. Are you all set to get it posted on Indeed and LinkedIn and social media tomorrow?"

Josh was silent for a moment.

"Okay, I can tell you're not thrilled with something I just said," Margaret went on. "And I know it's not the good news from Haversham. Did I miss a step in getting the job posting ready?"

"No," said Josh, "or, well, not exactly. But let me float one more idea by you. Margaret, from the requirements on the AGM job description, I think we have a couple of rock-solid internal candidates here in the hotel already. When is the last time that we promoted someone from within into leadership?"

Margaret thought for a moment. "You know, I can't actually think of the last time we did that. It's just that the internal folks don't have all of the experience that I would like and I'm not sure that I have the time to train someone!"

"Well, I would like to suggest that it would be a great way to live our new culture to look at our internal promotion possibilities first before we go to the outside," Josh said. "I think it will send a really powerful message about valuing the talents of the team if we provide them with career-growth potential. That is a big draw for lots of people if we can give them a career in the hotel—not just a job.

I understand that internals may need some development, but if you think about it, so will an outside candidate. While our internals may need some coaching and support on things like management skills or how to do certain tasks, they already have familiarity with the hotel and team, which is huge. We know these folks all fit with our culture too."

Margaret fiddled with her reading glasses. "Say more about that. Who did you have in mind?"

"Well, I think both Mark and Linh have great potential for the role. Mark has been with the hotel for almost ten years in the same job. He knows everyone and has a great handle on our guests. This would be a good move for him and a chance to get broader operational and strategic experience. He already manages a pretty big team in F&B."

"That makes sense," said Margaret. "And Mark already gets along well with both of us, so that seems workable."

"I also think Linh has done a great job in her role as director of sales and she really understands our market, which could make her a good AGM candidate as well. She's also a more strategic thinker than Mark, but she will need some help with her leadership style. She is pretty reserved and sometimes avoids possible conflict."

"I could see Linh growing into the position as well," said Margaret. "Especially now that we hired back Cherise as sales manager from that other hotel across town. She could step up into Linh's position within a few months, I'd imagine."

"Right. They both have some learning to do but we could provide them with the development opportunities that they need."

"What about the hard feelings that one or both of them will have when they don't get the job? Aren't we setting up a conflict situation then?"

"Not if we handle it well. If we present this properly, both of them will be flattered that we think so highly of them. It will be great recognition and validation for whoever gets the job, but it will also be a good opportunity to coach them if they don't get it. Besides, even if one of them does get the promotion, they will still need to work on some new skills in order to be successful. I've been wanting to introduce the concept of individual development plans—this would be a perfect launching pad for the idea."

"I might have known you had a whole new idea waiting to come out," laughed Margaret. "What's this one about?"

"Regardless of how the AGM job gets filled, we need to look closely at creating more formal career development opportunities for our employees," said Josh, some pride clear in his voice. "We both know it's an important part of our overall effort to provide a great end-to-end employee experience. I think one of the first strategic projects the new AGM could start with would be putting together clear career and competency paths for each department of the hotel. I'd help, of course, and there would probably be a Kaizen team, but it would be Mark or Linh's baby. This could improve our EX while giving the new AGM a project to grow into—*and* delegate some leadership work from both you and me. Everybody wins!"

Margaret couldn't help but smile at Josh's enthusiasm. "Okay, you've sold me on exploring the idea at least. Let's schedule meetings with Linh and Mark next week, and in the meantime, you can show me the details of this potential career path project. Sound good?"

"Definitely. I'll be up after lunch. This is going to be great."

The Solution

Providing career paths and professional development opportunities to your employees is an absolute requirement when creating a positive employee experience. We have heard some rather silly objections from leaders who don't want to invest in developing their staff because there is a chance that the employees will leave and take their training elsewhere and the hotel will "lose its investment." Consider the alternative—you don't help your employees develop new skills and they stay on with a less-than-ideal level of competency.

So, how does one go about creating career paths and development models for employees? It will take some effort and planning but once the ball gets rolling, the momentum will really pick up.

CAREER PATHS

The first step in creating a development culture is to define some logical career paths. This is a way to visually depict the career trajectory within a certain job family. For example, in housekeeping, it can be Housekeeper I, Housekeeper II, Housekeeper III, Housekeeping Trainer, Team Lead, Supervisor, and Housekeeping Manager. One of the key concepts here is to define different job levels so employees can see an upward movement opportunity. There is an incentive to learn more skills and recognition of efforts to do more. Seeing this path forward may help employees overcome the "it's not my job" objections from team members when you ask them to do something a little out of the ordinary.

When you are able to show this kind of career ladder to a new recruit, and to explain that there are pay increases that come along with these increased responsibilities, it demonstrates to your employees that they can find a career with the hotel—not just a job.

The differences in the first few levels—in this example, Housekeeper I, II, and III—can be fairly minor. It may be a function of time on the job, productivity (number of rooms cleaned per shift) as well as some level of cross-training for more-complex tasks. It is both a retention tool and a development tool for the team. We have attached a sample career path document at the end of this book.

Not every job in the hotel will lend itself to a career path—there may be some one-off type of roles that are hard to fit into this kind of structure. The goal with these is to talk about the skills and competencies needed for this role and for others, and help draw the picture of where else the employee can move within the hotel.

COMPETENCY MODELS

In addition to a defined career path, simple, straightforward competency models are critical. This helps hotel leaders describe what a successful employee looks like in their organization. This aligns with comments that we made earlier about clearly defining expectations. Competency models help tell employees what is expected at their level and at the next level. We have found it useful to utilize a step-up model for competencies—start with basic competencies that are required for all employees and then build up from there. As employees move up the career ladder, the competency expectations increase.

A simple competency model can look something like this:

LEADERSHIP COMPETENCIES
Strategic Thinking
Decision Making
Employee Development

MANAGER COMPETENCIES
Effective Delegation
Constructive Feedback
Conflict Resolution
Innovation

TEAM LEAD COMPETENCIES
Problem Solving
Strong Communications
Initiative
Understanding of Diverse Perspectives

CORE COMPETENCIES—ALL HOTEL EMPLOYEES
Honesty & Integrity
Service Excellence
Quality of Work
Teamwork
Respect

REGULAR 1:1 MEETINGS

The foundation of all effective career development planning is open and honest dialog between managers and employees. Supervisors and managers need to implement the practice of regular one-on-one meetings with their employees. Yes, it takes time out of your already busy day. However, it is essential in order to really understand the employee's interests and direction and functions as a vehicle to provide regular, constructive feedback to the employee. Together, you can discuss the employee's career path and how to get there.

Development is just one reason to do 1:1 meetings. The following graphic illustrates more about the importance of this practice.

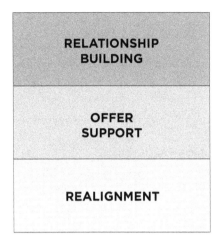

While regular 1:1 meetings can be incredibly powerful, poorly done ones can be a train wreck. Plan ahead for them and then actually DO them.

Best practices for effective 1:1 meetings include:
- Regularly scheduled—on the calendar

- Block the time and keep it—most of the time

- No distractions—go to a private area, put phone away

- Be curious—ask good questions (open ended)

- Share the air—listen

- Stay positive—lead the way

- Recognize their good work

A sample agenda for 1:1 meetings can look like this:

1. Start with recognizing a win (or great effort)

2. Employee updates you on current status (they talk, you listen)

3. How can I help you accomplish your goals? (barriers, resources, information, etc.)

4. You update on current & future issues (provide information)

5. What have you learned since we last met?

6. Do you have any questions for me?

7. Say "thank you!"

INDIVIDUAL DEVELOPMENT PLANS

Once a manager and employee have had some conversations around career path and professional development, it is important to make a plan to address gaps and to write it down. This is essentially what an Individual Development Plan (IDP) is. It is an intentional work plan for filling gaps in high-potential employees' career development to ensure that they are ready to take on new challenges and lead when asked.

Let's take a moment here to talk about the difference between high performers and high-potential employees. In some cases, they are one and the same. In others, they are not and it is imperative not to confuse the two. High performers are those folks who are really good at their current job. They do it well and achieve success. However, not in every case is this person ready, willing, and able to do more. Whether it's the steady Eddie who wants to just continue doing a good job in their current role, or someone who has the talent to do more but not the desire, there are just some employees who do not choose to advance. This is not a bad thing; every hotel needs these types of employees. They provide a solid base upon which to build.

It can be very tempting to just blindly promote the high performers but it can also be a dangerous practice. We have all seen examples of individuals who were promoted up past their expertise or level of competence. It usually is a failure and we risk burning out or losing a solid employee—who is now in a bad job fit.

For those employees with potential to do more, a well-crafted IDP is an important tool. It shows your confidence in them and it puts an action plan in place to assist the employee in growing into the next job. We have included an example of a simple IDP at the end of this book.

Key Elements

- Assessment of strengths and growth opportunities

- Prioritized focus areas (no more than two to four)

- Action Plan to build on strengths and to fill gaps

DEVELOPMENT OPPORTUNITIES

One of our guiding principles is that "professional development" is a shared responsibility. The hotel, the manager, and the employee all share accountability for each individual's development.

Development is more than classroom training or sending an employee to a seminar. Without a doubt, the most useful (as well as easiest and least costly) learning experience is on-the-job learning. *The Center for Creative Leadership* articulates effective professional development as comprising of the following three components:

1. **Seventy percent** of adult learning comes from experience (on the job assignments, task force, special projects, self-development, etc.). For example, this could be having the housekeeping team lead start doing the initial scheduling for the coming week. The manager can then review it and tweak as needed, along with a teaching moment around why the changes are needed.

2. **Twenty percent** of development comes from other people (job-shadowing, coaching and mentoring, leading by example, associations, etc.). An example of this can be encouraging a high-potential front desk agent to shadow a sales manager for a day or two to see if they are interested in transferring into the sales area. It can also involve encouraging supervisors and managers to become involved in local associations and business groups.

3. **Ten percent** of professional learning comes from coursework (workshops, classroom training, and webinars). This can be training that your hotel sponsors, workshops that are offered locally, or even additional coursework that may benefit the employee. We have often encouraged up and coming leaders to take a finance class so that they can more easily read financial statements and understand clearly how the hotel makes money.[11]

NOTE: You may need to clearly articulate to your employees that special assignments, shadowing, etc., are a part of their "career development" or else they may not assign that value to it. Connect the dots for them to ensure it happens.

---

11   "The 70-20-10 Rule for Leadership Development," Center for Creative Leadership, https://www.ccl.org/articles/leading-effectively-articles/70-20-10-rule.

MANAGEMENT TRAINING

The transition from a high-performing individual contributor to that of managing and leading other people is always a challenging one. It means moving away from using the technical skills and abilities that made one successful in the first place to working effectively through other people. Your success no longer results from just doing your job well, it now comes from how well your team performs. Managing and leading takes an entirely different—and often new—set of competencies.

Most people don't just become great managers/leaders without some assistance. Organizations can help make this transition smoother and more successful by offering some fundamental management training—skills-building to these budding and new managers. Teach them some techniques and provide them with some tools for HOW to effectively lead through others. It matters not if you bring this kind of training in house or if your find an external resource for your new leaders. It does matter that you provide access to this kind of skills building. Don't make the mistake of assuming that because the employee was a good Front Desk Agent, Engineer, or Sales Manager that they will automatically be an effective people manager.

Some typical topics for management training include:

- Effective hiring and selection methods

- Employment law basics

- Providing constructive feedback

- Creating a motivating work environment

- Delegation and accountability

- Understanding and respecting differences, unconscious bias

- Conflict resolution

- Change management

- Emotional Intelligence

DELEGATION

One of the toughest challenges for managers is learning how to delegate effectively. Too often, a manager may have learned to be successful based upon his/her own personal effectiveness and willingness to work hard. At some point, that is not enough. A really successful hotel leader needs to learn to use her/his resources—especially people resources—to the fullest potential. This means learning to delegate effectively.

Let us note this is not always an easy thing to do. The problems that we see come in when a manager assigns a task but is less than specific about the expected outcome. In this instance, the employee will accomplish the task by making assumptions about what "good" looks like. If that assumption does not match the expectation of the manager, then there is a big disconnect. The manager gets frustrated and questions the competence of the employee. The employee is upset at the "micromanaging" and feels that if the manager wanted the project done in a specific way, he or she should have done it himself or herself!

This is a case of delegation gone wrong—whose fault is that? We would say it is the fault of the manger who did not clearly delegate in the first place.

To figure out how to delegate properly, it's important to understand why people avoid it. Quite simply, people don't delegate because it takes a lot of up-front effort.

After all, which is easier: designing and writing content for a brochure that promotes a new service you helped spearhead, or having other members of your team do it? You know the content inside and out. You can spew benefit statements in your sleep. It would be relatively straightforward for you to sit down and write it. It would even be fun. The question is, "Would it be a good use of your time?"

While on the surface it's easier to do it yourself than explain the strategy behind the brochure to someone else, there are several important reasons that mean that it's probably better to delegate the task to someone else:

- First, if you have the ability to spearhead a new marketing campaign, the chances are that your skills are better used further developing the strategy, and perhaps coming up with other new ideas. By doing the work yourself, you're failing to make best use of your time. You likely become overloaded and focus on the wrong stuff.

- Second, by meaningfully involving other people in the project, you develop those employees' skills and abilities. This means that next time a similar project comes along, you can delegate the task with a high degree of confidence that it will be done well, with much less involvement from you.

Delegation allows you to make the best use of your time and skills, and it helps other people in the team grow and develop to reach their full potential in the organization. We have included a delegation model at the end of this chapter. Using this model *before* you delegate a task will greatly improve the chance of success.

We want to make an important note here—there is a key difference between good delegation and micromanaging. Delegation talks about WHAT needs to be accomplished, by WHEN, using what resources. It does not focus on HOW to do the work.

We all know that as managers, we shouldn't micromanage. However, this doesn't mean we must abdicate control altogether: In delegating effectively, we must find the sometimes-difficult balance between giving enough space for people working to the best of their ability, while still monitoring and supporting closely enough to ensure that the job is done correctly and effectively.

Take time to explain why they were chosen for the job, what's expected from them during the project, the goals you have for the project, all timelines and deadlines, and the resources on which they can draw. And agree on a schedule for checking-in with progress updates.

Last, make sure that the team member knows you want to know if any problems occur, and that you are available for any questions or guidance needed as the work progresses.

Delegation is a win-win when done appropriately, however, that does not mean you can delegate just anything. There can be a temptation to lighten your heavy workload by "dumping" less-desirable tasks on others to free up your time. Occasionally, this may not be a bad strategy as long as you recognize that is what you are doing. *However,* understand that these are not assignments that are motivating, will give your team a growth opportunity, or will expand the capacity of your team. Overdoing this may have negative consequences.

When you first start to delegate to someone, you may notice that he or she takes longer than you do to complete tasks. This is because you are an expert in the field and the person to whom you have delegated is still learning. Be patient: if you have chosen the right person to delegate to, and you are delegating correctly, you will find that he or she quickly becomes competent and reliable.

When delegated work is delivered back to you, set aside enough time to review it thoroughly. If possible, only accept good quality, fully complete work. If you accept work that you are not satisfied with, then your team member does not learn to do the job properly. Worse than this, you accept a bunch of work that you will probably need to redo yourself. Not only does this overload you, but it also means that you don't have the time to do your own job properly.

Of course, when good work is returned to you, make sure to both recognize and reward the effort. As a leader, you should get in the practice of acknowledging every time you are impressed by what they have done. This effort on your part will go a long way toward building team members' self-confidence and efficiency, both of which will be improved on the next delegated task; hence, you both win.

We have utilized a very effective framework for delegation on the following graphic.

Effective Delegation Framework—
Steps to "Doing It Right"

STEP ONE: Preparation Phase	STEP TWO: Planning Phase
Identify for yourself the goals of the work to be delegated, what needs to be done, and by whom. Identify the job to be delegated: • Results expected • Materials, information needed • Time frame • Other's resources Who the task will be delegated to: • Consider employee abilities, knowledge, interests & experience • Developmental goals • Consider employee's current work load	The employee who is chosen is briefed on the task to be completed. • Explain the task and results expected (*not how*) • Explain reasons for delegating to this person • Describe how the tasks fit into the larger picture of department • Talk about potential challenges • Talk about resources • Talk about authority level and scope • Establish check-points/ follow-up • Emphasize employee's responsibility and express your confidence (*Let go!*)

STEP THREE: Check-Point/Follow-Up	**STEP FOUR:** Completion Phase
Check on the progress of the assignment and make any necessary changes or adjustments. • Make sure all needed materials and resources are available to the employee • Discuss progress • Offer encouragement	• Accept the completed project and acknowledge the associate's efforts. • Do not accept unfinished, unprofessional, or off-target results. • Show an interest in the results and the experience that unfolded for them. • Talk about any "key learnings." • Recognize the employee. • Accept your own accountability. Do not blame the employee for less-than-satisfying results for which you may be responsible.

LEADERSHIP COACHING

At the more senior levels (such as the new AGM role at The Capitol House Hotel in our story), it may be beneficial to hire a leadership coach to help the new leader learn and practice targeted skills and habits. This type of coaching is laser focused and specific to the needs of the individual. A relatively small investment in a leadership coach can help the new leader develop a successful style more rapidly and with fewer missteps along the way.

CHAPTER TEN

THE RESULTS ARE IN

The Story—Three Months Later

Finally! thought Margaret, putting down the first draft of the report she was preparing for Haversham. *We've really turned the corner. And as much as I would never have wanted to admit it a year ago, I think much of the credit has to go to Josh. If he hadn't opened my eyes to how helpful some of these new changes would be, I'm not sure I would have gotten there.*

She took a sip of coffee, remembering how hard she and Josh had fought each other for the first few weeks of that year. *I'm so impressed with all the changes that have happened. And it really began with that first coat of paint in the employee break room, a few Kaizen teams, and simply listening to our employees.*

Josh knocked on the doorjamb, interrupting her reminiscing. "Hi, Margaret. I think we might only need a short meeting this week. Mark is really settling in to his new AGM role. I just got done reviewing the new F&B career trajectory plans with him and Cherise.

It is so fun to see him stepping up, and his and Linh's suggestion to have Cherise make the department jump to take his position was a genius idea."

"I do have to agree with that," Margaret nodded. "I am always impressed with the ideas that he is bringing to our weekly one-on-one meetings. Also, now that he and I have been working with that delegation model you showed me, I don't feel like I'm having to micromanage him at all."

Josh smiled. "I can't wait to see this month's report. Everything I've heard from the other department heads and my early data tells me that we've finally gotten a few months of positive trend lines behind us and hopefully we've really turned the corner. I know turnover is down, the early pulse from the GSS scores was solid, and according to the Linh, hopefully our STR numbers are the same."

"That's what I'm reading as well!" said Margaret, surprising her HR director with a high-five. "Also, I'm so pumped about the action teams that we put in place to respond to some of the feedback received from the employee engagement pulse survey. The ideas that the team is surfacing are outstanding!"

"You said it," said Josh. "It feels so great to finally be able to be proactive and to work on ways to improve the culture and the employee experience. This is what I was hoping to do when I got here."

"Yes. We've turned the corner for sure. And I completely agree, we have some good challenges ahead of us yet, but it feels great to be able to focus on the longer-term, important stuff rather than just fighting fires. Looking back, I really should have seen the signs before I had to be slapped in the face with them. The declining scores on our Team Member Surveys really was the first wake-up call; and I completely missed it. Haversham was right. The declining surveys lead to greater turnover. Greater turnover lead to decreased GSS scores that promptly led to declining occupancy, rates, and revenues. The significant change in our profitability was the natural outcome. Now, every one of these metrics is, while not perfect, trending in the right direction.

"Josh, I know I have said this before but I haven't said it enough. You and your ideas have been a big part of this turn around. I literally could not have done this without you. Haversham was not only right about the metrics, and he was right when he referred me to you." Margaret paused for a minute. "I have learned a lot about leadership and what people need in the past months. And if I didn't know it before I do now. People make or break this hotel and the most important part of my job as the GM is to support our folks so that they can do their best work. It is all about our people. Thank you for helping me learn that."

Conclusion

What we have learned throughout our leadership journey is similar to what Margaret and Josh discovered. Almost every problem that surfaced in the hotels had a people component to it. We have seen clearly that: Employee Engagement = Decreased Turnover = Increased Guest Satisfaction = Improved hotel metrics.

The utilization of Lean Continuous Improvement or Kaizen shows us that, until we dig into the issues and processes and really see the problems, we are mostly focusing on assumptions and symptoms. Too often we choose to jump forward from the problem to the solution without truly working through the process of looking at the root causes. Here we saw that the process of stepping back to see and map the entire process was key to finding the right solutions.

By digging into the processes as our characters did in the early chapters, we clearly identified the root cause of the problems we were facing and we were able to tackle the problems at the source, not the surface. While a surface glance told us that we were having sales or market share problems, a deep dive clearly identified that these were, at root, a "people" problem. Listening to the wisdom of the people who are actually doing the jobs—our employees are key. We needed to step back and take a look at the entire employee experience in order to fix the fundamental problems.

In fact, if there is one point out of this entire book we'd like to you to take away with you, it's to listen to your employees. As Bill Marriott Jr. put it in his book *Without Reservations:*

"Listening is the single most important on-the-job skill that a good manager can cultivate. A leader who doesn't listen well risks missing critical information, losing (or never winning) the confidence of staff and peers and forfeiting the opportunity to be a proactive, hands-on manager. Listening is also how you empower people to grow in their jobs and gain confidence as decision makers."[12]

As Margaret learned, change at Capitol House had to start with listening—first with herself listening to Josh, then the both of them listening to other employees, and finally with everyone in the hotel having ways to listen to each other. When no one was listening, turnover was high, performance was bad, and profitability was terrible. Once listening became a priority again, turnover dropped, performance picked up, and profit turned around.

Change leadership is a critical skill for every leader today. Hotel leaders must focus not only on identifying when change is needed but also how to best get there and how to influence others to embrace

---

12   J.W. Bill Marriott Jr., *Without Reservations: How a Family Root Beer Stand Grew into a Global Hotel Company* (Luxury Custom Publishing LLC, 2013).

the change. As we discussed in several of the chapters, communication is critical. In the absence of good information about what is really happening, people will make it up. And what they imagine to be true is almost always worse than reality.

As Margaret learned in this book, people are indeed our most important asset. Savvy hotel managers can no longer continue to treat employees as commodities. Instead, we need to look and improve the end-to-end experience that employees have in our hotels. We need to transform ourselves into a place where people enjoy working and want to stay. It's not about winning awards for being a great place to work (although they are nice and do help with recruitment), it is about becoming a place where the best people want to work.

In summary, we hope you will take away something that the two authors learned when we worked together; and that Margaret and Josh learned during their journey. Often, the solution is found during the journey and not at the end. In addition, we learned that "all of us are smarter than any one of us." It was the combination of Margaret's experience and Josh looking at the challenges from a different perspective that allowed them to find the solution. The true power of this partnership was exposed only after Josh and Margaret had learned that each of them was an asset—that both brought a significant strength to the table, and they began to trust each other and work together.

In closing, we remind you it's all about your people. Successful hotels have learned to shift their paradigms and stop focusing exclusively on the bottom-line metrics. When we create a powerful and positive end-to-end employee experience, we become an employer of choice for the best employees. The best employees provide a superior guest experience that results in increased profitability, guest satisfaction, and market share.

There is no single good answer for how to create a great employee experience. It takes dedicated focus, a commitment to continuous improvement and Kaizen, and the willingness to let your employees help guide you. You need to ask questions, listen with the intent to understand, and involve employees in designing the new world of work. Remember that what works for your hotel (and what makes you unique) will be somewhat different for another hotel. The employee experience concept is both challenging and worthwhile because it is driven by individual differences and preferences.

We have included many specific suggestions and ideas in this book—ones that we have seen work in various cultures. Our hope is that a few of them have resonated with you and that you can implement them in your hotel.

However, our ideal outcome is more than the specific suggestions or ideas that we have outlined. The key point of this book is that successful hotel leaders need to shift their thinking about their marvelous human capital and focus on finding, growing, and keeping the best of the best talent. Hotel managers need to be the change leaders who can visualize the change needed, communicate what success looks like, and build systems to support this vision. These leaders will find what works to engage and inspire their employees. These amazing team members will then make all the difference in the bottom-line results that your hotel will achieve.

This difference truly is "The People Effect."

2.1 Sample Code of Conduct for Hotel Employees

It is our intention to build and support an organization culture that treats all employees and guests as they wish to be treated. Fairness and respect, trust and integrity are the foundation of all that we do. In order to help our employees meet our performance expectations, and for them to be successful at The Capitol House Hotel, we expect the following from every employee:

Do the right thing. Capitol House Hotel employees are expected to follow the law in all situations. You should know and follow all company policies. If there are any questions about a policy, employees should ask their supervisor for clarification.

Treat all people with dignity and respect. This means showing respect for individual differences. This means no shouting and no name calling. This means no fighting or physical aggression.

Present a professional image—you represent the hotel. At Capitol House Hotel, most employees are assigned uniforms and are required to wear them during scheduled work shifts. Uniforms must be clean and un-wrinkled. Pants are not to drag on the floor. Individuals who do not wear uniforms are expected to dress profession-ally. All employees must wear a nametag whenever they are on duty.

Create a world class guest experience. Go the extra mile to help our guests—even if it is not in your job description. Make eye contact, smile, and greet every guest that you happen upon during your shift. Stop your conversation with other employees to acknowl-edge the guest immediately. Indicate that you will be with the guest as soon as possible if you are tied up in some way. The guests are your reason for being here, and their satisfaction helps ensure your success.

Show up when scheduled. Regular attendance and punctuality ensure even, efficient handling of daily business and makes life easier for you and your coworkers. In case of an emergency, tardiness, or sudden illness, call or text your supervisor at least *two hours* before your shift start time and keep him/her informed. If you are out more than one day, you must call or text your supervisor each day at least *two hours* before your shift start time.

Use company resources wisely. We all benefit when the hotel is profitable. Each of us has the ability to impact that every day in our jobs. Avoid wasting or misusing company resources.

Use technology appropriately. We recognize that most employees will have a smart phone with them and that it can be helpful in communicating within the team. When on duty, avoid any personal calls or texts except in the case of an emergency. Set your ringers to silent or vibrate.

When in doubt—ask. If any expectations, work processes or policies are not clear, you should ask your supervisor or any other member of the management team. Don't assume that you under-stand—we want you to be sure and clear.

Note: Violations of this code of conduct may result in disciplin-ary actions up to and including termination of employment.

2.1 More on Lean

https://www.lean.org/WhatsLean

2.2 Kaizen Team Charter Template

KAIZEN TEAM CHARTER

Name: _____ Date: _____

Problem Definition: _____

_____

Expected Outcomes/Improvements: _____

_____

Team Members:

Name	Role	Department

Resources Needed: _____

_____

Results: _____

_____

3.1 Performance Improvement Plan Template

Date:

To: **<EMPLOYEE NAME>**

From: **<MANAGER NAME>**

As we have discussed, I am concerned about your performance in a few areas. To address these concerns and to document a plan to get your performance where it needs to be, I am placing you on this Performance Improvement Plan (PIP). While on this PIP, your focus needs to be on satisfying the performance goals set forth below, and we expect immediate and sustained progress toward achieving the identified goals/objectives.

This PIP is not intended to identify all performance expectations for any particular period of time. Rather, this PIP highlights areas that we have currently identified as requiring your particular attention. I expect that you will not only meet or exceed the expectations set forth in this PIP, but that you will meet or exceed all expectations required of someone with your position.

PERFORMANCE IMPROVEMENT PLAN REQUIREMENTS

My primary concerns regarding your performance are as follows:

Improvement Opportunity	Current State	Action to be Taken

I believe these are very attainable goals. My expectation is that we will, at a minimum, have weekly progress meetings to document progress relative to achieving the performance metrics set. I expect you to initiate scheduling and the agenda for these discussions.

Duration

This PIP will remain in place until we conclude that you have satisfied the specific expectations set forth below. I will regularly evaluate your progress under this PIP over the next thirty days and will advise you at the end of that period of time whether you have satisfactorily complied with the expectations and requirements set forth in this document.

Consequences

You must show immediate and sustained progress toward achieving the identified goals/objectives. I expect that at all times you will comply with the expectations and requirements included in this PIP and will perform your duties in a manner that is consistent with your position. Failure to do so could result in further disciplinary action, up to and including termination of employment.

At Will Employment

This document is not a contract for employment and does not change the "at will" status of your employment with the hotel. This means that either you or the hotel may terminate your employment for any reason at any time, including at any time during the PIP period identified above.

Acknowledgements

My signature below indicates that I have read and understand the information contained in this Performance Improvement Plan.

Signed: _____ Date: _____

Supervisor: _____

Employee Comments: _____

_____

_____

_____

10-day Follow-up:

Signed: _____ Date: _____

Supervisor: _____

Employee Comments: _____

_____

_____

_____

20-day Follow-up:

Signed: _____ Date: _____

Supervisor: _____

Employee Comments: _____

_____

_____

_____

30-day Follow-up:

Signed: _____ Date: _____

Supervisor: _____

Employee Comments: _____

_____

_____

_____

4.1 Respectful Workplace/ Preventing Harassment Questionnaire

RESPOND "TRUE OR FALSE" TO THE FOLLOWING STATEMENTS AND BE PREPARED TO DISCUSS YOUR RATIONALE.

1	Only women can be sexually harassed.	True ____	False ____
2	Harassment can occur between members of the same sex.	True ____	False ____
3	An individual's perception determines whether behavior or actions are offensive.	True ____	False ____
4	To be considered sexual harassment, the action or behavior must be sexual in nature.	True ____	False ____
5	The company is not liable if the alleged harasser is a vendor or contractor.	True ____	False ____
6	It's okay to tell a coworker of the opposite sex that he/she looks nice.	True ____	False ____
7	To be considered workplace harassment, the harasser must be a supervisor.	True ____	False ____
8	Harassment only occurs at the workplace during actual work hours.	True ____	False ____
9	Behavior will not be considered harassment if the person saying/ doing it is has cultural standards that are different.	True ____	False ____

		True	False
10	If everyone else is ok with a coworker's behavior, you should accept it even if it bothers you.	——	——
11	If you ignore harassing behavior or bullying, it will ultimately stop or go away.	——	——
12	If someone lets you know that your behavior makes them uncomfortable, you should stop that behavior immediately and not engage in it again.	——	——
13	If you do not intend to offend anyone and you "mean well," your behavior will not be considered harassment.	——	——
14	Members of management cannot legally ignore complaints of sexual harassment or keep the information to themselves.	——	——
15	A supervisor can guarantee complete confidentiality once a complaint of sexual harassment is made.	——	——
16	Asking a coworker out on a date is sexual harrassment.	——	——
17	Sexual harassment cases can result in significant individual as well as corporate liability.	——	——
18	It is illegal to retaliate in any way against and employee for complaining about or reporting workplace harassment.	——	——

19	The victim does not have to be the person harassed but could be anyone affected by the offensive conduct.	True ____	False ____
20	Organizations cannot be held liable for a supervisor's unfulfilled threats.	True ____	False ____
21	It's ok to share or joke when it's "just the guys" or "just the girls."	True ____	False ____
22	Manager-employee romances are illegal.	True ____	False ____
23	It is only a problem if the disrespect-ful behavior is face to face.	True ____	False ____
24	Sexual harassment is less about "sex" and more about POWER.	True ____	False ____

5.1 Pulse Survey Sample Guidelines

GOALS:

These quarterly pulse surveys are designed to engage our employees and provide insights in order to:

1. Attract, retain, and motivate a high caliber of employees.

2. Provide input to leadership about opportunities for improvement.

3. Ensure that we are acting in a manner that is in alignment with our values and culture.

SURVEY DESIGN:

Quarterly pulse surveys can be modified to address current situations or needs. In general, the surveys will be 6-8 questions with 2-3 as standards for every survey in addition to 4-5 questions regarding the quarterly focus.

For example:

Q1 focus area = Overall engagement

Q2 focus area = Leadership/communication

Q3 focus area = Compensation, benefits, and extrinsic rewards

Q4 focus area = Career and professional development

Rating scale – the survey statements will have five possible responses ranging from 1) strongly agree, 2) somewhat agree, 3) neither agree nor disagree, 4) somewhat disagree or 5) strongly disagree.

STANDARD QUESTIONS MAY INCLUDE (PICK 2-3):

- ☐ I take pride in working for this hotel.

- ☐ I have confidence in the future of this organization.

- ☐ There is a promising future for me in this hotel.

- ☐ I intend to work for this hotel for a long time.

- ☐ I have at least one colleague at work who I consider a friend.

- ☐ I find my job challenging and interesting.

- ☐ I feel respected at work.

- ☐ This company treats employees well.

- ☐ I trust the leadership of this hotel.

ENGAGEMENT FOCUSED STATEMENTS (PICK 4-5):

- ☐ There is a positive culture at this hotel.

- ☐ I am recognized when I do excellent work.

- ☐ My work gives me a feeling of personal accomplishment.

- ☐ My company inspires me to "go above and beyond" my normal job duties to help the company succeed.

- ☐ My works gives me a sense of personal accomplishment.

- ☐ I am able to use my strengths in performing my job.

- ☐ Our values guide how people at my company actually behave.

- ☐ Teamwork is encouraged at this company.

- ☐ I know how I can contribute to the hotel's success.

LEADERSHIP/COMMUNICATION FOCUSED STATEMENTS (PICK 4-5):

☐ Overall, my direct manager is doing a good job.

☐ Senior leadership shows a sincere interest in employee well-being.

☐ Leadership communicates effectively.

☐ Employees are kept well informed about issues facing the hotel.

☐ There is a strong focus on customer service in my company.

☐ My direct manager listens to my ideas and suggestions.

☐ I receive feedback from my manager/supervisor that allows me to improve my job performance.

☐ The expectations of work performance are reasonable for someone in my position.

☐ Leadership/management has a high degree of honesty.

☐ I am involved in making decisions that affect my job.

COMPENSATION, BENEFITS, AND EXTRINSIC REWARDS FOCUSED STATEMENTS (PICK 4-5):

☐ I am paid fairly for the work I do.

☐ My total compensation package is competitive in our industry.

☐ I have the tools and resources that I need to do my job well.

☐ I know that if I perform well in my job, pay increases will come.

☐ The health insurance benefits offered by my hotel are competitive with what other, similarly sized companies offer.

☐ The amount of paid leave is competitive with what other, similarly sized companies offer.

☐ I am happy with the physical working conditions at my job.

☐ I feel that I have good job security.

CAREER AND PROFESSIONAL DEVELOPMENT FOCUSED STATEMENT (PICK 4-5):

☐ I receive the training I need to do my job well.

☐ I understand my role in this hotel.

☐ New employees get the training they need to perform effectively.

☐ I feel I have an opportunity to grow professionally within this hotel.

☐ There are opportunities for me to focus on my professional development.

☐ I have the opportunity to learn new things and develop new skills in my role.

5.2 Two Way (Skip Level) Meeting Outline

PURPOSE:

1. To provide an opportunity for direct, two-way conversations between hotel employees and senior leadership of the hotel. Our goal is to make sure that the hotel continues to be a good place to work.

2. To provide an opportunity for hotel leaders to interact directly with hourly staff to ensure that they have the support and tools that they need in order to be successful in their roles.

GROUND RULES:

Confidentiality. No comments will be passed back to your management. We will aggregate the feedback. Same rules for you—don't give someone a hard time for anything they say.

Honesty. We are looking for open and honest feedback from you.

No topics are off limits. We may not be able to fix everything you bring up, but we can still talk about it.

DISCUSSION QUESTIONS

1. Tell us what you like about working for this hotel.

2. Has the hotel changed during your time here? If so, how?

3. How do you let the managers know about your ideas?

4. How can we make it easier for you to do your job?

5. What are your ideas for how to improve the guest experience?

6. What else do you want to talk about?

6.1 Employee Referral Program

WHO DO YOU KNOW THAT WE SHOULD KNOW?

The Capitol House Hotel needs a few more great people. Our occupancy is up, we have events on the books, and the hotel is rocking the competition. That means work for us. That's where you come in! We need your help finding great new people to join the Capitol House team.

Our best source for new employees is you—refer people that you know. Look through the positions we post on the Hotel intranet and think about the people in your network (LinkedIn, Facebook, and Twitter) and make that referral. Who do you know that we should know?

To up the ante and to reward your efforts, The Capitol House is increasing the amount we pay for employee referrals for *difficult to staff positions* for the next several months. An employee who refers someone that leads to a hire of a new housekeeper, front desk agent, or banquet server will receive **$300**! Referral of a Sales Manager candidate will pay you **$500**.

So, how does that work? Just refer your friends, neighbors, or acquaintances and have them list you as the referring source or let us know directly. If we hire them, you will receive a check for 50 percent of the total referral amount on the first pay period after the new employee starts. Once the referred employee successfully completes three months of employment, you will receive a second check for the remaining 50 percent.

Interested in learning all the nitty gritty program details? Keep your eyes open for candidates you want to work with here at The

Capitol House and send your referrals to Josh in Human Resources today. Thanks for helping us grow.

6.2 Draft business card for referrals

FRONT:

LOOKING FOR A FEW GOOD WOMEN & MEN

THE CAPITOL HOUSE HOTEL
ADDRESS, EMAIL AND PHONE

BACK:

- Come and join our team

- We have the following open positions:
    - Housekeeper I
    - Front Desk Agent II
    - Engineer
    - Sales Manager

- Please call 404-123-4567 or
- www.joinus@thecapitolhousehotel.com

IT'S MORE THAN A JOB!

It's challenging

It's fun

It's great friendships

It's creating great guest experiences

It's never dull

It's an opportunity to learn & grow

It may be just right for you!!

7.1 Writing Effective Job Ads

HOW TO WRITE AN AD THAT DETRACTS TALENT

The Front Desk Manager's primary responsibility is to assist the General Manager in achieving the hotel's long-range profit and revenue goals by directing the operations of the Guest Service Department. This position is responsible for ensuring hotel consistency in quality of standards, as well as the delivery of outstanding guest service and effective operations primarily of the front desk. The Front Desk Manager is also responsible for selecting, training, evaluating, developing, and motivating the Guest Service Representatives and the Breakfast team.

HOW TO WRITE AN AD THAT ATTRACTS TALENT

Dynamic team is ready for a dynamic leader. Award winning hotel is seeking to add one more outstanding player to a stellar lineup!

Winning skill sets will include:

- Coach

- Mentor

- Revenue Maximizer

- Communicator

Get ready for the next step! Our managers don't just achieve, they excel! You will be joining a team that helps prepare you for the next stage of your career. The Front Desk Manager of today is the General Manager of tomorrow!

8.1 Creating a New Hire Checklist Template

The following is a template that can be used to create a new hire checklist. We have included some sample checklist items for reference.

Category	Task	Accountability	Completed (Supervisor & Employee initials)
Welcome	• Manager calls new employee upon acceptance of job— express your pleasure and how you look forward to working together • Announce new hire to rest of the team		
Timekeeping	• Show the employee how to clock in and out		

Category	Task	Accountability	Completed (Supervisor & Employee initials)
Schedule	• Explain schedule • Discuss overtime requirements • Review required meetings • Discuss call-off procedure • Review time off requirements/ process		
Guest Service Expectations	• Discuss guest interaction expectations		
Job Duties	• Provide job description • Review Code of Conduct		

Category	Task	Accountability	Completed (Supervisor & Employee initials)
Work Environment/Uniform	• Provide access pass/keys • Provide name tag and uniform • Describe uniform and hygiene requirements		
Safety	• Provide PPE • Watch required safety videos		
Socialization	• Arrange for someone to have break or lunch with new employee on first day. • Identify a peer buddy for the new employee		

Category	Task	Accountability	Completed (Supervisor & Employee initials)
Training			
Other			

8.2 Life Skills Training Curriculum

- Work Ethics (Attendance, Accountability, Acceptance, and Appreciation)

- Resume Writing

- Interviewing Skills

- Communication Skills (Verbal and Non-Verbal)

- Decision Making Skills

- Overcoming Obstacles

- Financial Literacy (Depending on Client Request)

- Brand Affirmation (7 Principals from Customer Service)

8.3 Basic Hotel Training Curriculum

- Customer Service Certification
- Front Desk Certification
- Restaurant Server Certification
- Guest Room Attendant Certification
- Maintenance and Facilities Certification
- Kitchen Cook Certification (Prep) if Kitchen is available
- Tourism (Ambassador) Certification
- ServSafe Certification
- TIP's Certification
- OSHA 10
- National Retail Certification

9.1 Training Resources

https://www.ahlei.org/Programs/AHLEI-Programs/

9.2 Individual Development Plan Template

Name: _____ Date: _____

Current Role: _____

Where do I want to move in my career? _____

_____

_____

_____

Indicate below the key focus areas for individual development.

ACTION PLAN

Specific Skill I want to develop	Learning activities/ actions I will take to develop these skills	Start and end date	I will know I have achieved my goal when:

Employee Signature: _____

Direct Manager Signature: _____